MW00678858

PRACTICAL ADVICE FOR PRINCIPALS

ALBERT LEE SNOW

A SCARECROWEDUCATION BOOK

The Scarecrow Press, Inc.
Lanham, Maryland, and Oxford
2003

A SCARECROWEDUCATION BOOK

Published in the United States of America
by Scarecrow Press, Inc.
A Member of the Rowman & Littlefield Publishing Group
4501 Forbes Boulevard, Suite 200, Lanham, Maryland 20706
www.scarecroweducation.com

PO Box 317
Oxford
OX2 9RU, UK

British Library Cataloguing in Publication Information Available

Library of Congress Cataloging-in-Publication Data
Snow, Albert Lee
  Practical advice for principals / Albert Lee Snow.
    p. cm.
"A ScarecrowEducation book."
  ISBN 0-8108-4594-6 (pbk. : alk. paper)
  1. School principals—United States—Handbooks, manuals, etc, 2.
School management and organization—United States—Handbooks, manuals,
etc. I. Title.
LB2831.92 .S59 2003
371.2'012—dc21
                            2002014995

To my parents, Glenn and Dolores, for giving me an appreciation for reading and a life-long love of knowledge and learning, and my wife, Angie, for helping me to pursue my dreams and goals

CONTENTS

INTRODUCTION

According to a 1998 study by the National Center for Educational Statistics, 93% of school principals in the United States were over forty years old. In 1999, the National Library of Education reported that 40% of practicing principals were almost ready for retirement. In these constantly moving and ever-changing times that we live in today, being a school principal has become a very complex and demanding business. Principals are expected to fill many different roles and be an expert in all of them. A principal is supposed to be a disciplinarian, an instructional leader, and a manager and to maintain a school with the most outstanding standardized test scores around. A principal's work-week usually consists of five full work days plus three or four nights of additional duty per week. Because of all these factors, many principals are deciding to leave the profession. The Association of California School Administrators developed the following information:

> Principals report that high stress, time demands of the job, broadening demands of the job that far exceed salaries, and new state accounting legislation make retirement appealing. Add to that the shortage of teachers— the primary pool from which principals emerge—and the impending administrator crisis should become a national concern. (Kerrins, 2001)

The need for principals will only grow more acute in the near future. Currently, 40% of the country's 93,200 principals are almost eligible for retirement, according to the National Library of Education. As a result, the U.S. Bureau of Labor Statistics estimates that school administrator job openings will rise 20% by 2005 (Curriculum Review, 1999).

From all of this, it is obvious that there is going to be a continued need to train new administrators. This book is intended to provide practical administrative strategies for new and practicing administrators.

When I became a teacher, the most valuable experience I had in my preparation for the teaching profession was my directed student teaching, in which I actually taught in a high school classroom. Unfortunately, nothing gives you as true a picture of the realities of the job in training principals the way that student teaching does for teachers.

Many states, however, do not train principals for the real-life situations that they will face in their initial positions. For example, when I first became an assistant principal my only training besides my teaching experience was five graduate courses in educational administration. I don't recall any of those courses preparing me to handle all of the discipline problems of a thousand-student high school. Needless to say, I learned a lot of things the hard way and I am sure there are many principals out there learning in the same manner. This book should provide some guidelines for principals in carrying out their day-to-day responsibilities that may not have been covered in their graduate educational leadership classes.

A good friend of mine became a principal a few years before I did. We went to high school, college, and graduate school together. We had also taught at the same junior high as first-year teachers. I can still remember his description of his first day as a school principal. It was summer and he was the only person at the school. He looked around at his unfamiliar surroundings and said to himself, "What do I do now?" Hopefully, what follows will help to answer that question.

This work is based on my own experiences as a principal in public and private schools on the elementary-, middle-, and high-school level. I have incorporated some of my own research and the research of others into this text. First and foremost, this is a book written by a practicing principal for other practitioners or aspiring practitioners.

1

A PRINCIPAL'S DAILY DUTIES

A principal is very simply defined as the head of a school. In today's public and private schools, the title and role of principal cover a lot of territory. Subsequent chapters will focus on the following principal roles: the principal as instructional leader, the principal as disciplinarian, the principal as personnel manager, and the principal as public relations officer.

This chapter deals with the day-to-day duties of a principal—tasks that aren't always stressed by educational leadership professors, but should be performed on a daily basis.

STRATEGY #1

Be the first one there and the last one to leave.

This very simple strategy can make or break a principal. If teachers are to report to school at 7:30 A.M, the principal needs to be there at 7:00 A.M. If teachers leave school at 3:00 P.M., the principal needs to stay until 4:00 P.M. Arriving at work before the rest of the staff is valuable for several reasons. First, teachers appreciate seeing the principal at school when they get there because it gives the impression that the principal is on the ball and gets things done. How a principal is perceived is extremely important. Image may not be everything, but the perception that a principal is not on the job can be very damaging to the school as a whole. Second, principals cannot expect teachers to be at school or on duty on time if they are not. Also, I have observed a tendency among some teachers to be jealous of the higher salaries paid to administrators. Arriving early and staying late can help alleviate some of the criticism that accompanies this jealousy. It is much better to hear comments like "I wouldn't have your job because of all the extra time you are on duty" than it is to hear comments like "Principal Jones sure has it made."

Staying after the children and teachers leave also creates several advantages for principals. Again it gives the impression that the principal is committed and responsible, but it also says other things as well. For example, students often have problems at school, but they don't say anything until they get off the bus at their house. Parents immediately call the school to complain or just check on the situation. Major problems can sometimes be avoided if the principal is available at these off-peak hours. You may not be able to do anything about the situation at the time, but you can assure the parent that you are on top of things—which is all many people want to know anyway. Also, the principal should stay until all bus routes are completed. Students, mostly elementary students, often get on the wrong bus or miss their stop. Principals need to be around to help with these situations. Ideally, principals should have the capability to contact each bus by cell phone or radio. If you have ever dealt with a mother who can't find her first grader, you know what I am talking about.

STRATEGY #2

Be at all school functions.

Strategy #2 is a corollary of Strategy #1. If a school has a function of any kind, the principal needs to be there. This can be one of the most demanding, time-consuming aspects of a principal's job, but there is no way around it. Appearances at school functions are mandatory for several reasons. Security is always a concern. At ball games, for example, fights could break out or there could be a power outage. There are countless situations that could occur that an administrator would need to deal with. I once had to cancel a ball game because of severe weather conditions brought on by an unexpected and fast-moving hurricane. The principal being at school functions can also improve the atmosphere or climate of your school. Students appreciate the fact that the principal cares enough about them to show up at their games or band concerts. Not only do the students appreciate this, but the parents like it too. Teachers also are glad to see administrators support the extracurricular activities that they sponsor.

The number of functions or night and weekend duties a principal is responsible for is directly proportional to the age of students. The younger, elementary school students have fewer functions the principal will have to attend; the older, high school students have more. High schools have the most night and weekend assignments because of the large numbers of ball games and social events, such as the prom or the homecoming dance. If a school has a principal and one or more assistant principals, the duties may be shared. However, the principal should still go to as many events as possible, even if it is just to make an appearance. This can be one of the burdens of school administration. It helps if you truly enjoy being around young people. It also requires a little bit of planning sometimes to ensure that you have a home life too. Finally, if you are just making an appearance, make sure everyone sees you. I always have the public address announcer introduce me at each event, just to let everyone know that I am there and on the job.

STRATEGY #3

Return all phone calls.

Returning phone calls sounds very simple, but in practice it can be difficult to implement and may require that you set aside a specific part of the day to get this done. Again, this is a perception thing. If a principal returns telephone phone calls in a timely manner, that principal is perceived as having his act together. The opposite of this is also true. I once failed to return the call of the state superintendent of education. I never got his message, but that didn't help me after the state superintendent mentioned it to my local school district superintendent. I was perceived as being lax in supervising my office staff, and my office was seen to be unprofessional and disorganized. Believe me, that is not the kind of reputation a principal needs. If you have a problem with staff not delivering messages, replace those staff members. This and other personnel issues will be discussed further in Chapter 2.

STRATEGY #4

Walk the campus before school.

Campus inspection should be the first task a principal performs every day on the job. Once you arrive at school, take a few minutes to organize your thoughts for the day and then walk the halls. The walk allows the principal to inspect the facility for various defects, such as break-ins, vandalism, graffiti, leaks, and broken pipes. Second, the walk enables you to see the teachers as they arrive and for them to see you. It is important that teachers see that they are being supervised from the time they arrive on campus until the time they leave. Teachers are more apt to arrive and depart in a timely manner if they know they are being monitored by their supervisor. Teachers, like most people, sometimes need the presence of a superior to remember their duties. Monitoring of teachers' schedules can be varied by standing in the teacher parking lot at sign-in time or standing in the office with the sign-in sheet in your hand.

Walking the campus also allows the principal to greet students as they come on to the campus. When students know they are being observed, they are less likely to act up. It also helps to set a positive tone for the day. If students congregate in one area before school, the principal needs to be seen in that area to lessen the chance of any discipline problems occurring. At this time the principal can also ensure that all staff are at their duty stations to alleviate some of the principal's responsibility to supervise students. Administrators and teachers should always work together to monitor and discipline the students.

STRATEGY #5

Be in the hallways during all breaks and class changes.

When the bell rings to change classes, principals should patrol the halls. If students congregate in one particular area, the principal should help to supervise that area. The principal's presence in the hallway between classes and during breaks helps to reduce the number of discipline problems at these peak times. Many major discipline problems, such as fighting, occur during these transition periods, and anything you can do to reduce the number of these occurrences makes your job easier and your school safer. I have avoided dozens of potential fights or conflicts simply by being seen by opposing groups.

An added benefit is that you can also use this time to supervise your teaching staff. Since it is impossible for two or three administrators to supervise a school full of students by themselves, teachers must also be responsible for student supervision. It is the principal's duty to ensure that teachers fulfill these supervisory duties.

STRATEGY #6

Walk the campus after school.

There are several major areas that need to be monitored by teachers or other staff immediately after school is dismissed: the hallways, the bus pick-up area, and the student parking lot. The after-school walk is one way of ensuring that duty teachers and/or security guards are on the job as assigned by the principal. If you have assistant principals, assign them to specific, high-visibility areas since the mere fact that principals are visible helps to alleviate discipline problems. Also, the after-school tour gives teachers or other staff the opportunity to talk to the principal about general questions or concerns. However, if staff have major requests or problems, it is wise to get them to write it down to avoid confusion. Teachers like to see the principal around the campus, so it is important to be present around campus as much as possible.

STRATEGY #7

Communicate with students, teachers, and parents on a daily basis.

Lack of communication can be a major problem for principals. Numerous problems can be avoided if all the different groups involved with a school are regularly kept informed. The following suggestions for communication have been performed in schools for years, but that does not make them any less important. Communication needs to start before the school year kicks off by publishing the school-year calendar in the local newspaper. Also, make sure that the calendar is included in the student handbook that you give to each student on the first day of school. The student handbook is also a good place to publish all of your school's team sports calendars. Schedule questions are the most frequently asked questions in the school office. It is also important to ensure that each child and/or parent confirms receipt of the handbook in writing. This can be done by including a tear-out sheet in the handbook for parents to sign and return. The parent's signature eliminates any discrepancy that may occur in the future. Once the school year starts, the principal should see that monthly and weekly calendars are distributed and, if possible, published in the local newspaper.

Daily communications, both written and oral, are also important. Announcements made over the intercom should be limited to the first thing in the morning and right before students are dismissed at the end of the day in order to avoid interruption of class time, unless absolutely necessary. Interruption of classes is often construed by teachers as disrespectful and disruptive. If the school has closed circuit television capability, try to use it when possible as it is an effective way to communicate with the entire student body. Written announcements should go out once a day with the absentee report. The administrator should also ensure that these announcements are kept on file to avoid any future complaints of non-receipt.

Finally, keep your teachers informed of all activities as often as possible, including upcoming events that disrupt the normal routine. Written memos are a good tool to help remind teachers or announce new additions to the school-day schedule since we all have busy schedules and sometimes forget about or misplace the school calendar. Teachers want and need regular contact with their administrator, and it is the administrator's job to keep them informed and updated.

Don't forget about special programs and then suddenly announce a change of schedule at the last minute. I forgot the snake man one time. Try telling a guy with thirty snakes you forgot to put him on the schedule. Mistakes like that can ruin your image as a competent principal with a well-run school.

STRATEGY #8

Get out of your office of much as possible.

Being a principal requires that you spend a certain amount of time in your office every day for a variety of reasons. For example, Strategy

#3—return all phone calls—requires a certain amount of office time on a daily basis. The principal is also the chief financial officer in most schools, which alone consumes a great deal of time. Every principal has to personally sign countless purchase orders and budget requests and attend various meetings with parents and teachers. If you let these responsibilities control your day, you can get trapped in your office. While budgeting and financial responsibilities and meetings with parents and teachers are all very important, they must be balanced with classroom observation and campus tours. If you stay in your office all day, teachers and students will soon get the impression that they are not being supervised, which can become problematic. As previously mentioned, teachers, like most people, sometimes need the presence of a superior to remember their duties. Not enough supervision leads to increased discipline problems. Save yourself some trouble: *Get out of your office.*

STRATEGY #9

Remember that you are totally responsible for your school.

Strategy #9, being totally responsible for the school, is not part of a principal's everyday concern, but the principal should always be cognizant of the overall well-being of the school. All school issues, ranging from poor test scores to a discipline problem at the ball game on Friday night, are the principal's responsibility. This applies to both the good and the bad. Harry Truman coined the phrase "the buck stops here." Nowhere is that more true than with a school principal. More and more states are making school districts, individual schools, and principals accountable for their student's academic performance. The following is an example of the increase of accountability of principals in California.

The Academic Performance Index [API] is the centerpiece of the public schools accountability system and the new measuring stick for California schools. . . . With the first API scores now in and the rankings for individual schools listed in newspapers and the Internet, it is critical that principals and district administrators . . . develop specific plans to meet their API growth targets for next year and beyond . . . schools that meet their growth targets may be eligible for cash and non-monetary awards from the state. Under-performing schools that fail to improve may be sanctioned. (Weis, 2000)

Some principals may actually be removed from their positions because of this new focus on test scores and accountability, so that is a major area of concern. In addition to test scores, the principal is also responsible for the school having a safe and orderly climate. If the school has discipline problems, the principal is held accountable. The principal is also responsible for supervision of teachers. If a teacher is doing a poor job in the classroom, it is the principal's responsibility to improve the situation.

Being a school principal in these times is a demanding and complex job. The responsibilities are tremendous. One should be aware of these responsibilities and evaluate them seriously in the decision to become a school principal.

STRATEGY #10

You are the principal—act like one.

This particular strategy, acting like a principal, covers a lot of territory. What does it mean to act like a principal? It means just what it says. A school principal is a public figure like a minister, a politician, or the local chief of police and should act accordingly. Your school's community has certain expectations of what a principal should be. Respectable,

trustworthy, reliable, conservative, and honest are just a few of the ad-
jectives that come to mind. It is your job to try to live up to those expectations, which means you should always act as though you are representing your school, because you always are. Don't buy beer at the
local convenience store where all the students hang out. Old administrators used to talk about the " three county rule": If you want to go out
and have drinks, do it at least three counties from where your school is.
Keep your personal life private as much as possible. Now, many of you
are thinking that your personal life is no one's business but your own. If
you are a school principal, your public behavior and conduct will be
scrutinized.

Some of these things may not apply if you do not live in the community where your school is located. Not all of these suggestions are mandatory but rather recommendations for being a successful and respected
principal. Church attendance is also highly recommended. Remember,
the way you are perceived in the community depends on how you are
seen behaving in the community.

STRATEGY #11

Make decisions.

One's decision-making ability is essential to maintaining a positive
reputation with parents, students, and teachers. Principals must make
decisions quickly and often under stressful conditions, which requires
good judgment, experience, training, and common sense. If a principal has trouble making decisions, he or she is perceived as weak and
ineffective. Ideally, one should attempt to get input from various
groups and consider all sides of a problem. However, you don't always
have that option as many decisions must be made immediately and under duress.

One of the keys to being a successful principal is involving all relevant parties, such as students, teachers, parents, and the community, in the decision-making process as often as possible. Research indicates that, when teachers have input on matters that affect their working conditions, organizational learning is increased (Marks and Louis, 1999). In some states, such as Kentucky, some decision making has been taken away from principals and given to school-based, decision-making councils (Klecker, Austin, and Burns, 2000). As a principal, I find this decision-making process problematic as it removes the administrator from the equation. Most principals have been trained in decision-making procedures and are crucial to the process as a result of this knowledge and experience. Furthermore, if a principal is held totally responsible for a school, as suggested in Strategy #9, then he or she should play a major role in the decision-making process.

The following are a few general recommendations for decision making:

- Try to think through all possibilities thoroughly first before making any decision.
- Never do anything that cannot be justified in a reasonable manner.
- Talk things over with the assistant principal(s) if possible.
- Always remember: You are responsible. If you are not prepared to sit down and defend your decision to a parent, child, or the school board, don't do it.

There are formal decision-making models that can be used to help principals make decisions. Examples of these are the Vroom-Yelten Decision Process Model, the Vroom-Jago Model, and the Maier Model (Ubben, Hughes, and Norris, 1997).

STRATEGY #12

Dress appropriately.

When parents, teachers, and students come to school, they expect to see a principal who looks like the principal. It should be clear to all parties that the man in the coat and tie or the lady in the professional-looking suit is the principal. Harry Wong has this to say about dress: "Make no mistake, we judge others by their dress and they judge us too. It may not be fair. It may not be right. But people tend to treat other people as they are dressed. It's common sense. You will be treated as you are dressed. As you are dressed, so shall you be perceived; and as you are perceived, so shall you be treated" (Wong and Wong, 1998). As administrators, we should always adhere to high standards of professional dress and demand that our staff dress appropriately as well.

STRATEGY #13

Stand up for your staff.

Standing up for staff is extremely relevant to the staff's opinion of their principal and their position in the school. Faculty and staff need to feel that the principal is their advocate and supporter. Nothing hurts morale more than for a staff to feel they aren't supported by the administration. Don't let parents, students, or other teachers harass, belittle, or demean your staff. Under no circumstances should anyone be allowed to direct profanities or vulgarities to staff members or put their hands on staff members. If an irate person is giving a teacher a hard time, the principal needs to intervene and either diffuse the situation or remove the belligerent person from the school grounds. Your teachers deserve this from their principal. I once had to physically remove an irate parent who threatened violence to my 5'3" teacher. That is part of the principal's job. These situations can often be avoided; but if they occur, don't be afraid to contact security.

There is, however, another side to this strategy. Teachers need to know that they will not be supported if they are in the wrong. Teachers are not perfect people and they need to know that if they do something wrong they will be held accountable or even reprimanded. Principals cannot support unreasonable teachers who are unable to justify their actions. A general rule to follow is: don't do anything as a principal that cannot be explained in a reasonable manner to a student, parent, teacher, superintendent, or the school board. I follow this rule and I expect my teachers to adhere to the same standard. It is a good idea to make teachers aware of your beliefs regarding support and discipline before school gets started.

If a teacher needs to be corrected or reprimanded, don't do this in front of parents if at all possible. Personnel matters should be handled between the principal and teacher, not in public.

STRATEGY #14

Ask yourself, "What have I done for the children at my school today?"

Reflection and reflective writing are an integral part of becoming a nationally board-certified teacher and should be something administrators do on a regular basis. Administrators sometimes lose sight of the fact that every action taken at a school should be performed with the best interests of the children in mind. The question itself may sound amusing to some, but our job is to teaching children is and it should always be our number-one priority.

I know a school superintendent who asks his principals that question on a regular basis. What have you done for the children today? That is one way to keep focused on the education of children. Take a few minutes each day to focus on what you are doing and how it helps children learn. The question can be answered in several ways. "I disciplined two students who were disrupting a math class. This allowed the rest of the children in that class to concentrate on the lesson without interruption." "I conducted a staff development session that provided teachers with some new teaching strategies." "I made sure my teachers were on their duty posts to promote a safe and orderly school climate that is conducive to learning." Principals need to take the time to reflect on this question frequently to keep themselves focused on the true mission of their school.

STRATEGY #15

Ask your teachers, "What have you done for your students today?"

This strategy is directly related to Strategy #14. Not only do administrators need to reflect on their actions, but they need to ensure that their teachers stay focused on educating the children. Again it sounds a little funny: "What have you done for your students today?" But if you think about it, this is what education is really all about and teachers need to be constantly reminded of that.

SUGGESTED ACTIVITIES FOR CHAPTER 1

1. Keep a time log of your activities for a week.
   a. At the end of the week determine what activities take up most of your day as a principal.
   b. Keep track of the strategies from Chapter 1 that you have used each week.

2. Share how you would answer the question in Strategy #14, "What have I done for the children at my school today?"

3. Share how some of your teachers answered the question in Strategy #15, "What have you done for your students today?"

4. Discuss how you communicate with your staff.

5. Discuss how you as a principal are affected by Strategy #9.

6. Give examples of decisions that you have to make on a daily basis.

All of these questions can be used as written assignments, part of a portfolio assessment, or as group discussions or projects in a workshop or class setting.

2

PERSONNEL

There are three key elements to a school: administration, teachers/personnel, and students. Other elements, such as parents, facilities, and the community, all have an influence on a typical American school but are not key elements for a principal. One of a principal's main responsibilities is to hire, fire, manage, and supervise all of the certified (teachers and counselors) and noncertified (secretaries, bookkeepers, custodians, security guards, and cafeteria workers) staff. People's perceptions of the quality of a school come, in large part, from their dealings with school personnel. This is why the way a principal handles personnel is such an integral part of their success as an administrator.

STRATEGY #16

Hire high-quality teachers.

Other than academic achievement and discipline, one of the most important areas of responsibility for a principal is the hiring and firing of teachers. The quality of teachers is directly proportional to the quality of instruction taking place in a school. It is getting harder and harder to find experienced, professional teachers. Not only do schools need to hire more teachers due to increasing enrollments, but there are also significant numbers of young teachers leaving the profession early in their careers (Hope, 1999). Retirements also play a major role in the difficulty of finding high-quality teachers:

> An estimated 70,000 instructors retired from their public schools this fall. That represents only around 2% of the nation's 2.7 million teachers, but one in three of remaining educators have been in the classroom for 20 or more years and are on the verge of qualifying for retirement. In fact, the Education Department forecasts that almost a million teachers will retire over the next decade. ("What the numbers say," 1999)

What this means for principals is that the pool of qualified applicants is shrinking. The ideal candidate for an open teaching position has a current state license in the advertised area, a master's degree in the field, and four to five years of teaching experience. It has been my experience that applicants possessing those qualifications are few and far between. More likely the candidate will have no experience and not even have his or her teaching license in order. Why schools of education allow these students to graduate without proper licensure is beyond me. To be fair to teacher education programs, many states are responding to the shortage of qualified teachers by establishing alternative routes to teacher certification. This movement has spread across the United States and is intended to get people with training in specific academic fields, but no training in education, into the classroom. This enables professional people who want to become teachers into the classroom with the theory that their knowledge of their particular field will make up for their lack of formal training in education.

Many universities and colleges across the country have developed programs to accommodate these nontraditional aspiring teachers. Some of these programs, like the one at Old Dominion, provide extensive hands-on experiences in the classroom while other provide only a few weeks of summer training. Graduates of these latter programs claim they are underprepared to teach, and many of them leave the profession quickly (Bassinger, 2000). In my opinion the alternate certification route is used by many young, aspiring teachers as a means of avoiding student teaching. Student teaching is possibly the most valuable training a young teacher is exposed to. If you hire alternate-route teachers, be aware that you will be basically providing them with on-the-job training. Alternate-route teachers may not have set foot in an elementary school, middle school, or high school since they themselves were students. In my experience, alternate-route teachers have varying levels of success: Some have been good teachers, and others I have let go by Christmas.

As principal, what can you do to have qualified professional people in your classrooms?

1. Try to get experienced teachers, or at least ones that have completed student teaching.

2. Do not take the first candidate who has the right qualifications. Try to interview as many applicants as possible.

3. Check references. This is a must. Try to contact as many former employers as possible. You do not want to hire someone else's problem.

4. Have structured, formal interviews.

5. Get input from your staff before making decisions about hiring. It is still your final decision, but getting teacher input is a useful team-building technique.

6. Have a police background check done. You do not want to find out in the paper or the local television news that you have hired a convicted felon.

Another area that needs to be addressed is that of salary and benefits. Schools are often limited by state mandate in the salary they can offer prospective teachers. However, if at all possible, school districts and states need to make teachers' salaries and benefits as attractive as possible. This is the only way we are going to attract and keep the best and brightest teaching candidates. I have worked in school districts where teachers could drive a few miles and make thousands of dollars more per year for the same duties. The difference in salary definitely makes it much more difficult to retain good teachers. When I tried to address this problem with a school board member, I was told "If money is a consideration, we don't need that kind of teacher." This is the kind of mindset that will alienate good teachers and make it hard to keep a quality staff.

STRATEGY #17

Supervise your teachers. Be in the classroom as much as possible.

To have an effective school, teachers and students must constantly be engaged in the learning process. The emphasis of time on task is nothing new. "Processes in the real world take time; learning is a process. Learning takes time. . . . The more time that is spent actually learning a subject the more that is learnt" (Fisher and Berliner, 1985, p. 311). It is the principal's responsibility to ensure that teachers are making the most effective use of time in their classrooms as possible. An excellent way to ensure that teachers are carrying out their responsibilities is for the principal to physically be in the classroom observing what is taking place. Schedule part of your day for classroom observation as much as possible. In the old days, teachers might not see a principal all year unless they had some sort of problem. That type of leadership style just won't cut it today. As previously mentioned, teachers can be just like students: if the person in charge is not around things tend to get lax. An added bonus is that the students also see more of the principal, which tends to make the students behave better. Teachers and students need to know that the principal may show up at anytime.

One of the main methods used in teacher observation is the Clinical Supervision Model. This model consists of:

1. A pre-observation conference

2. The observation

3. Analysis of observation

4. Supervision conference

5. Post-conference analysis (Goldhammer, Anderson, and Krajewski, 1993)

There are also various techniques that can be used in the observation portion of the clinical supervision process. The Wide Lens Approach is probably the technique most often used by principals in classroom settings. Using this method, the principal keeps an anecdotal record of everything observed in the classroom by writing short descriptive sentences. These notes can record such items as teacher behavior, student behavior, and content of instruction (Atcheson and Gall, 1997).

The Verbal Flow classroom observation technique is a method of observation that records who is called upon and who responds to questioning. Principals can also keep a record of the physical movement of a teacher in the classroom as a method of observation. This method will tell you if a teacher is spending too much time sitting behind his or her desk (Atcheson and Gall, 1997). This is something I always stress to my teachers: Get up and teach. If the teacher is sitting behind their desk all day, there is not much teaching going on—just ask Harry Wong, a leading authority on the education profession.

Another observation method easily used by principals, involves observing the four pedagogical moves: structuring, soliciting, responding, and reacting. This can be done with a simple, four-column chart. The principal simply places a mark in the relevant column each time the teacher exhibits one of these behaviors.

There are various other techniques that can be used to observe different aspects of classroom instruction. Some of these other techniques are:

- Selective Verbatim
- Seating Chart or SCORE
- Timeline Coding
- Script Taping
- On-task Observation (Atcheson and Gall, 1997)

Some of these techniques are more appropriate for different situations. For example, if a teacher is having discipline problems, it would be appropriate to do an on-task observation to see if that might be the cause of the behavior problems. For a complete description of the Clinical Supervision Process and all other observation techniques, see Atcheson and Goldhammer (Atcheson and Gall, 1997; Goldhammer, Anderson, and Krajewski, 1993).

STRATEGY #18

Assign all teachers duty.

Almost all schools in the United States, in order to maintain a safe and orderly climate, must utilize teachers to help supervise the campus. It is the principal's responsibility to ensure that this happens. In my experience, there are some private schools that do not require supervision duties of teachers. These schools operate on an honor code philosophy in which students are expected to simply behave or be expelled. Principals don't have that luxury in the public setting. All society's children are entitled to a free, appropriate, public education in this country, and we essentially accept any student who comes through the door.

Typically in most schools, the number of administrators is determined by the number of students enrolled and the availability of funds in the district. The number of principals per school may also be mandated by the individual state. For example, the state or school district may say that there must be one administrator for every 500 students. According to that system, a 1,500-student high school would have three administrators (two assistant principals and one principal). While these are just minimum standards, it would still be virtually impossible for even ten administrators to supervise 1,500 students successfully. Therefore it is imperative that teachers have duty assignments. The following are areas that usually need supervision before and after school:

- Student parking lot

- Bus unloading area

- Hallways

- School entrances

- Any area where students congregate

Some of these areas require more than one supervisory person. Also, teachers should be assigned duty positions during breaks and class changes. Most of this supervision can be accomplished simply asking teachers to stand outside their classroom door between classes. Some areas, such as bathrooms, also require teacher supervision. Teachers hate this and you can't blame them. Nobody went to college to do "potty patrol," but if you want to stop smoking and other infractions from taking place these areas must be supervised. It is important to stop bathroom smoking as it is harmful to both the student who is smoking and to any other person using the bathroom.

Principals must remember that assigning teachers' duties has both a positive and negative: Teachers will not be happy about extra duties, but the increased safety and security of the school is well worth it. If you are limited by contract as to the number and types of duties that can be assigned, you may need to look at ways to eliminate the need for so much teacher supervision. Reducing duties can increase teacher morale, which is always a good thing. Some examples of alternatives to using teachers for supervision are:

- Using parent volunteers

- Using aides and paraprofessionals

- Issuing walkie-talkies to teachers near problem areas such as restrooms and staircases

- Limiting the number of lunch periods

- Closing areas of the campus to students before school, after school, and at lunch (Potter, 1997)

Once duties are assigned, the principal must hold teachers accountable by checking on them. (See Strategies #5 and #6 for more information on monitoring the campus.) As Potter contends, "A visible administrative team reassures the staff and reminds students of who is in charge" (1997).

STRATEGY #19

Hire professional office staff.

"Good secretarial help allows the educational leaders and their assistants to use their professional talents in improving the educational program"

(Wood, Nicholson, and Findley, 1985). This statement speaks to the idea that the role of secretarial and office staff is to free principals and teachers from the paperwork that can take time away from their main focus: the education of the children. Assisting with paperwork is just one of the many benefits of a quality office staff.

Since the school office is sometimes the only part of a school that some people see, it is extremely important that the office staff always acts in a courteous, helpful, and professional manner. When parents, or anyone for that matter, come through the office doors, they should be greeted by a member of the office staff and be dealt with as soon as possible. As principal, I always ask people in the office if someone is helping them. This does two things: It impresses people that the principal would take time to help them and it reiterates to the staff the importance of this aspect of their duties.

A professional office staff can also help a principal by addressing the concerns of a potentially problematic parent before they reach the principal's office. A good secretary can serve as a buffer by calming irate parents before the principal has to see them.

A couple of last words about office staff. If you are out of your office, instruct your staff to say "Mr(s). —— is out on campus. How may I help you?" This is a small item but it enhances the image that you are out supervising your school and taking care of business. Office staff should never say things like "I don't know where Mr(s). —— is" or "I can't find him/her." These statements can leave the caller with a negative impression, which is the last thing a principal needs.

STRATEGY #20

Get to know all staff members.

Upon accepting a principal's position, one of the first priorities is to find out something about your new staff, both professionally and socially. In the case of a new principal, this process should start before the first day of school. One way to start this process is to hold staff meetings with small groups of teachers. These meetings serve two purposes. First, these small-group staff meetings allow the principal to get a feel for his new staff and the staff has the opportunity to form their first impression of the new boss. Second, the principal can use these meetings to find out what the staff feels are the problems facing the school, both large and small. The teacher's perceptions are often different from those of the district superintendent, the school board, or the community. The principal can also use the staff's actions or attitudes in these preliminary meetings to develop theories as to who might need more development or supervision.

The next step in this process is for the principal to visit classrooms, talk to teachers on duty, and eat lunch with different groups of people. By doing these things, a principal can determine how to successfully supervise each teacher. Some teachers need a great deal of supervision while others need very little. Different teachers may thrive on additional tasks and responsibilities, while others are barely able to handle their specific teaching duties. Constant interaction with teachers also makes the principal aware of personal events that can affect a staff members performance. This does not mean that the principal should be everyone's best friend since principals must remain somewhat aloof from their employees. It means having enough personal knowledge of employees to effectively manage them.

STRATEGY #21

Remember employees' birthdays.

This is a very simple strategy that can pay big dividends. Have your secretary keep a list of all of the school employees' birth dates and send them birthday cards. Do this for everyone from your assistant principals to your cafeteria workers and custodians. Don't leave anyone out. It only takes a few seconds to write a message on a card, but this simple act shows your employees that you have taken the time to keep up with them on a personal level and shows a more human side to the boss.

STRATEGY #22

Allow employees time to take care of family matters.

Absenteeism is a problem in many school districts in the United States. Paying for substitute teachers can cost a school district thousands of dollars each month that could be better spent elsewhere. For this reason, it is necessary to set limits on the number of leave days taken or some teachers, often the weaker ones, will abuse the system. Substitutes just do not provide the quality of instruction that the regular teacher should. However, don't be so strict that you antagonize your employees over legitimate needs. For example, some school districts have a policy of only granting personal leave for the death of an immediate family member. A teacher in one of these districts requested a leave day to attend the wake and funeral of a distant relation who was a close personal friend. The request was denied with the response " And just how are you related?" This is a ridiculous example, but true. Why would you antagonize an employee like that? *Allow employees to take care of family matters.*

The school business is a "personal" business by nature. Education, from a management standpoint, should not be run like some gigantic, impersonal, multinational conglomerate. Sure, absenteeism can be a problem; but deal with those employees who abuse the policy on an individual basis through evaluations and, if necessary, terminate those with serious problems. Allow employees to deal with family and personal problems. This attitude will provide the principal with a more satisfied, more loyal staff.

STRATEGY #23

Hand deliver all paychecks to your employees.

Once a month take the time to walk the hallways of your school and hand deliver each and every one of your employees their paycheck or paystub. Following are a variety of excellent reasons for doing this:

- The principal has personal contact with each of the school's employees in a single day.

- The staff appreciates the principal taking the time to personally deliver each paycheck.

- The principal has another opportunity to briefly observe every single classroom in the school on the first or last day of the month.

- The principal is following Strategy #8—get out of your office of much as possible—and Strategy #17—supervise your teachers. Be in the classroom as much as possible.

- The staff is reminded that they are there to do a job, which they are paid for, and indirectly that this is their livelihood.

STRATEGY #24

Assess teachers' "fair share."

There are numerous activities that go along with the functioning of modern schools in this country besides just teachers teaching in their classrooms. On the elementary-school level this can mean PTA meetings, Christmas programs, field days, and many other things. On the secondary-school, middle-school, and high-school levels, there are countless football, basketball, softball, soccer, tennis, and baseball games. In addition, there are band concerts, debates, quiz bowl contests, beauty pageants, and student council functions associated with the school. These events require supervision not only by the administration but also by other school staff members.

First, there must be coaches and faculty sponsors for these activities to take place. Without a sponsor, for example, there would be no student council. Without a coach there would be no football team. Many of these positions carry additional pay supplements, but these supplements usually do not come close to compensating these people for the extended hours they put in. It can be difficult to find good people to fill all these positions. So, when you do find good people to take on these extracurricular duties, accommodate them as much as possible in order to keep them. Take away a duty or give them a good planning period. There are ways to do accommodate staff that do not cost a lot of money.

Coaches and faculty sponsors are the most obvious staff positions that are needed, but there are many others and this is where the rest of your staff comes in. As an example, look what goes into hosting a single basketball game at your school. Other than the coach, someone needs to sell tickets, run the game clock, keep the official scorebook, and maintain a safe and secure environment. That is at least five people and possibly more. For football games this number would probably at least double. If possible, pay a staff member to perform each of these duties. If you cannot pay someone to perform these duties, assign them to staff members on a rotating basis.

Some teachers generally just want to teach their particular class and go home and usually do not want to be involved in any of these activities. That kind of attitude is not good for the school climate as a whole. Teachers need to do their "fair share." Otherwise you wind up with a handful of employees doing all of the extra duties, which is not healthy for your staff and can lead to burnout of your good teachers. Also, all teachers need to connect with students on other levels besides just academics. I once observed a valedictorian from a major national university trying to teach high school science. This young teacher had a lot of problems relating to the students until the principal assigned the additional duty of being assistant soccer coach. The teacher became more successful after being forced to deal with the students on a different level.

For all of the aforementioned reasons, make these additional duties part of your evaluation process. Ask your teachers, "What have you done to help this school function besides teach your class?" There are a variety of ways to answer this question, but the important thing is that all teachers do something extra.

STRATEGY #25

Document all personnel actions.

One of the criticisms of education in this country is that there are many poor or incompetent teachers in the nation's classrooms. Another aspect of this is the public's perception that tenure, teacher organizations, and unions make it difficult or even impossible to get rid of poor teachers. It is the principal's responsibility to ensure that all members of a teaching staff are teaching to the best of their ability and teaching the students in a fair and consistent manner. If teachers are not carrying out their responsibilities, the principal must take steps to address the issue. First, inform the teacher of his or her deficiencies. Second, the principal must provide training to help improve the deficient teachers performance. If the teacher still fails to improve, disciplinary action of some type must follow. One school district was having a problem with some teachers being consistently late for work. After a handful of teachers were suspended from school for a day without pay, the teacher tardiness problem suddenly cleared up. That is a drastic measure, but drastic measures are often needed when teachers fail to act like employees, like all other workers in this country.

In order to dismiss a teacher for incompetence, these are some of the steps that must be followed and documented in writing by the principal. If a teacher is told to improve on "time on task," for example, put that in writing and have the teacher sign it. If you reprimand a teacher for not being on duty, put it in writing and have the teacher sign it. Once you get enough of these documented discipline actions against a teacher, it is not difficult to dismiss or not renew a teacher's contract. Always remember to document all your personnel actions; this allows you to remove poor teachers from the classroom.

Another factor to consider is that teachers are entitled to "due process of the law." Most states have statutes that govern the nonrenewal or termination of teachers. The most important part of this is that the teacher is entitled to a hearing, at which the teacher has the opportunity to refute the charges made against him or her. In these hearings, events from past years can be used as evidence against a teacher, allowing administrators to establish patterns of behavior and making it all the more important to keep your documentation in order (Reutter, 1994). *Don't be afraid to let go of poor performing teachers; it can be done.*

SUGGESTED ACTIVITIES FOR CHAPTER 2

1. Interview a principal and discuss hiring practices used by that principal.

2. Conduct a phone survey of local school districts to see how personnel decisions are handled. Is there a personnel director and staff, or are all hiring practices conducted by the principal?

3. Interview a personnel director, either from a nearby school district or a local business.

4. Critique two noneducation journal articles on supervision of personnel.

CHAPTER 2

5. Obtain a copy of a school duty assignment roster to share with the class.

6. Conduct an evaluation of your school office staff. List good qualities and deficiencies. Make a list of recommended changes.

7. Describe a practice used by a principal that helped that school's principal and staff connect on a personal level.

8. Discuss how extra duties for teachers were handled at a school where you were employed.

ACADEMIC IMPROVEMENT

For some years now, there has been a movement in the United States to measure the instructional quality of schools by scores on standardized tests. Some states are strictly using national standardized achievement tests such as the Iowa Test of Basic Skills (ITBS), the Stanford Achievement Test (SAT), or the Metropolitan Achievement Test (MAT). Other states have developed their own made-to-order tests. Texas has the Texas Assessment of Academic Skills (TAAS), Kentucky has the Kentucky Core Content Tests, and Mississippi has developed its own Grade Level Testing Program with the help of CTB-McGraw Hill. The effect of this emphasis on testing has been amply documented:

> The attention given to achievement test scores and the tacit implication that student test scores provide an accurate index of educational success helped fuel an enormous preoccupation with these scores during the last decade. School boards demanded that their district educators improve students' test performances. School administrators at all levels were evaluated almost exclusively on the basis of students' scores on standardized tests. And more than a few governors pinned their political aspirations directly to the elevation of their states test scores. California Governor Gray Davis, for

example, made the improvement of test scores so central to his administration's success that he publicly proclaimed he would forgo any bid to seek the U.S. presidency if his state's scores failed to rise. George W. Bush made Texas's rising test scores a central element in his successful presidential campaign. Now in 2001, there's no question that a score-boosting sweepstakes has enveloped the nation. Who has been tasked with boosting test scores? Teachers and administrators, of course. (Popham, 2001, p. 12)

This is the reality that we as administrators and teachers are facing as we take the educational process into the twenty-first century. There is not a school principal in the United States that is not concerned about raising test scores. Pressure to improve test scores comes from a variety of different groups including the national and state governments, state departments of education, neighboring communities, and your own school board and parents. An example of state pressure is the statewide report card, which is used by many states to rank the schools on various criteria and publish the rankings in the state newspapers. States also have different levels of accreditation in which schools are ranked on scales of 1 through 5 or 1 through 10. Competition for these high rankings can be fierce, and some districts devote most of their time and energy to trying to raise these rankings. I have seen principals and superintendents almost come to blows and principals and teachers get fired or reassigned over these rankings.

On the local level, for example, high school ACT score averages are listed in the local newspapers like a ball game score. The district with the highest average ACT or SAT scores is seen as the top academic school district in the area. These scores are also compared with the state and national average. Of course one average score should not determine how schools are perceived, but that is often how the general public sees things. As an example, West County High School has the best average ACT/SAT test scores in the area; therefore West

County High School must be the best school around. The newspaper doesn't publish the fact that West County only encourages their top students to take the test, while the other schools tested the entire junior class. Do you see how test results can be skewed in favor of one school over another?

Some states give every high school student the same test in certain subjects, such as biology, american history, English, and algebra. Many states require high scores on these subject area tests to graduate. Even without the requirement to graduate, don't think these tests aren't important. School board members call superintendents and ask "Why aren't our American history students' scores as high as the district next door?" When school board members call superintendents, superintendents call principals, and so on. These high-stakes tests can cause a great deal of stress for current administrators and are one of the contributing factors to principals deciding to leave the profession.

Again, these are the realities that we, as administrators, are forced to live with. The following are basic strategies that any principal can implement to help improve their schools academic performance.

STRATEGY #26
Set specific schoolwide goals for the year.

Setting a school goal of improving test scores or academic achievement is simply too general. Schools need to set specific goals. For example, in a middle school the students may be tested on math and language arts skills. The seventh-grade math teachers may set the goal of improving their math scores from the previous three years and can then develop strategies to help them achieve this goal. More staff development and additional class time devoted to mathematics are some possible strategies that could be implemented. Many schools at the middle-school level have doubled the time spent on mathematics and language arts to improve students' skills in these areas. One good method for increasing time spent on math and English is to change to some form of the block schedule as opposed to the traditional six- or seven-period school day schedule. On the block schedule schools can devote 90 to 100 minutes to math and English for the whole school year at the middle-school level. In an effort to improve students' math and reading skills, elementary schools have increased time spent on these subjects as well.

It is the principal's responsibility to guide the staff in improving test scores. Make sure that teachers facilitate the process by analyzing the problems themselves. Another source principals need to be aware of is the district-level curriculum specialists—take advantage of their expertise and advice. Principals often tend to try to do everything themselves. To improve academic performance, you can use all the help you can get.

STRATEGY #27

Provide quality staff development for your staff.

Since the 1980s, there have been many efforts to improve education in the United States. One of the most common efforts has been through staff development. Richard Dufour says, "it should be more apparent than ever that the best hope of genuine, significant school improvement lies not in state mandates or manipulation of graduation requirements, but in the development of the full potential of the professional staff within our schools" (1991, p. 5–6). Dufour also makes the following four points concerning staff development:

1. The local school district and school provide the best arena for school improvement.

2. School improvement means people improvement.

3. The principal is a key figure in determining the ultimate success of any effort to develop school personnel and thus plays a major role in school improvement.

4. Schools seeking meaningful improvement must make a commitment to staff development programs that are purposeful and goal directed.

States and school districts have handled staff development in various ways. Many states mandated that local school districts conduct a specified number of staff development hours per year. Some states had specific topics, such as using technology in the classroom, that school districts were required to address. The school districts themselves have implemented staff development programs in a variety of ways. Additional days have been added to the length of teachers' contracts specifically for staff development. Teachers are required to stay after normal school hours so many days a month for staff development. Some districts even have early release days for students so the teachers can have time for staff development.

No matter when you take the time to have staff development, there are some guidelines to follow:

1. Staff development should be part of a plan.

2. Topics should be related to your goals for school improvement.

3. Try to make the process as stress free as possible for teachers.

4. Staff development presenters must be interesting and dynamic.

5. Use your own teachers as resources and presenters as much as possible.

6. Try to give teachers some incentive for attending staff development sessions.

7. The principal needs to attend as many sessions as possible so that the teachers see that it is important to him or her also.

8. If the principal is not behind the program, the teachers won't be either.

STRATEGY #28

Have a plan for improving test scores.

The pressure placed on principals to see that their school's test scores meet the state and local authorities' standards can feel overwhelming at times. The task is much less daunting if one properly plans for the improvement measures. There are several ways to implement a plan for improving test scores. The first step is to identify the areas that need the most work and determine which grade levels or subject areas are experiencing the most difficulty. This needs assessment can be accomplished through a cooperative effort of teachers, guidance counselors, district test coordinators, district curriculum specialists, and administrators.

Once the areas needing improvement have been identified, the next step is to come up with a plan of improvement. There are several different methods for this also. Schools can set up committees to decide what strategies they are going to use to attack the problem. This process is similar to that described in Strategy #26—set specific schoolwide goals for the year. The improvement plan can also be developed using the federal government's program called Comprehensive School Reform Demonstration (CSRD), which promotes research-based school reform with an emphasis on academic improvement. Federal grants are available to implement school reform programs that meet the requirements set forth by CSRD. The components of this model are as follows:

1. Effective research-based methods and strategies

2. Comprehensive design with aligned components

3. Professional development

4. Measurable goals and benchmarks

5. Support within the school

6. Parental and community involvement

7. External technical support and assistance

8. Evaluation strategies

9. Coordination of resources (Mississippi Department of Education, 2001)

There are also a variety of educational resource companies that have developed programs that fit the CSRD requirements. These companies usually also provide assistance to schools in writing the actual grant proposal. Some of the major improvement programs being used in various states are these:

1. Accelerated Schools Project

2. High Schools That Work

3. Target Teach

4. Modern Red Schoolhouse

5. Success for All

6. Onward to Excellence (Education Commission of the States, 1999)

A more complete listing of these programs with detailed contact information can be found in the appendix to this book. This is not intended to be a commercial for any of these programs. If your school is not currently using one of these programs, do some research and investigate them yourself. Remember that none of these programs has any hope of success unless you can enlist the support of your faculty and parents. If you receive the support of these two groups, positive school change can take place no matter what program you eventually decide to use.

STRATEGY #29

Keep current with educational literature.

Not only is it important for the principal to provide quality staff development activities for the school staff, but it is also important for the principal to participate in staff development designed for administrators. Staff development for administrators should be provided by both the local school districts and the state departments of education. Many states require administrators to take a certain number of hours of courses, seminars, or workshops during a specific time period. Principals should use these opportunities to keep abreast of current issues, trends, techniques, and research in education. However, these activities take time away from school and often incur travel and other expenses. One of the easiest, most cost-effective, and least time-consuming ways to keep current in educational thought is to belong to professional education organizations and take advantage of their literature. Here are some examples of these professional organizations:

- The National Association of Secondary School Principals (NASSP), which publishes the *NASSP Bulletin* and *Principal Leadership*
- The National Association of Elementary School Principals (NAESP)
- The Association for Supervision and Curriculum Development (ASCD), which publishes *Educational Leadership*

- Phi Delta Kappa, an association of professional educators, which publishes *Phi Delta Kappan*, an excellent source on school reform

- The American Association of School Administrators, which publishes *The School Administrator*

Another good source of information for busy administrators is *Education Digest*, which condenses articles from other educational journals. School administrators also need to join state organizations like the Texas Association of School Administrators and the Association of California School Administrators.

Principals need to stay current with new ideas in education. Current administrators do not want to be like the old principal who liked to say he had thirty-five years of experience when he really only had one year of experience repeated thirty-five times.

STRATEGY #30

Check lesson plans every week.

As a first-year teacher, I was not always well prepared for my teaching duties and it showed. My first principal came around looking for my lesson plans and was not happy with the fact I did not have any. I didn't realize it at the time, but the simple act of being forced to sit down and think through my plan for the week made me a better teacher by making me more organized, efficient, and on task. Principals have been checking lesson plans for decades. Schools of education at our universities and colleges still emphasize the use of lesson plans. Mary Clement, an assistant professor of Education at Berry College in Georgia agrees, explaining that, "In my class, they learn how to teach and my syllabus begins with a unit on lesson planning" (Clement, 2000). Just because it is a strategy that has been around forever doesn't mean that it is not a valid tool to improve academic performance in the twenty-first century.

As I mentioned earlier, new teachers often do not see the need for planning out their activities on a regular basis, which is a recipe for failure. The old cliché is "people don't plan to fail, they just fail to plan." This is true for some new teachers, especially alternate-route teachers who did not major in education. It is the principal's responsibility to supervise teachers, and checking daily lesson plans is one way to do this. Another point to remember is that once the lesson plans are turned in, the principal needs to actually look at them and make written comments so that the teachers know they are being read. Nothing turns teachers off quicker than the idea that they are spending time making out lesson plans that no one is paying attention to.

New teachers today have an advantage that teachers did not have twenty years ago. There are numerous Internet sources, such as Edhelper.com, that teachers can access with ready-made lesson plans designed for their class. Textbook companies often have websites that offer sample lesson plans to reinforce the material in their texts. The Ask Eric Virtual Library (http://askeric.org/Virtual/Lessons/) and the Gateway to Educational Materials (http://www.thegateway.org/) are two excellent sources of lesson plans in many academic areas (Morgan and Sprague, 2000).

Lesson plans are also a good way to track teachers' implementation of certain state-mandated benchmarks or activities. Some states and school districts require integration of vocational activities into regular educational classrooms or integration of technology into the classroom. Lesson plans can be used to ensure that teachers are implementing all of these things properly. Even though it is an old concept, checking lesson plans is still a useful and valid strategy for today's principal.

STRATEGY #31

Mentor first-year teachers and poorly performing teachers.

At the start of each school year, assign a mentor teacher to all first-year teachers and teachers new to the school or district. Many new teachers leave the profession within the first few years, making it important that novice teachers be paired with a "master" teacher to help them succeed in their early teaching experiences. Twenty-five or thirty years ago, first-year teachers were handed a textbook, told to cover the entire book, and shoved into a classroom. In this new century, schools need to do a better job orienting and developing new faculty members.

Mary Clement (1995), while she was the coordinator of the Beginning Teacher Program at Eastern Illinois University, developed the following guidelines for the mentors of new teachers:

- Help the new teacher find things (supplies, etc.).
- Make resource books and magazines available (Wong's, *The first days of school*, etc.).
- Share workable ideas for communicating with parents.
- Share classroom management plans.
- Share strategies for teaching diverse students.
- Update the new teacher on what's new and what's working.
- Let the new teacher know that it is okay to ask questions.
- Model positive coping and stress relief strategies.

It has also been the practice in many school districts to place beginning teachers in the toughest teaching assignments or to give them the extra duties that no one else wants. There are two ways to look at this practice. Some educators say that young teachers are the only ones who have the strength and enthusiasm to handle the tough assignments, while others say that giving new teachers the worst assignments is the reason so many beginning teachers leave the profession ("Should new teachers," 2000).

Don't lose sight of the fact that one of the keys to a successful school program is hiring and retaining high-quality instructors. Anything you can do as an administrator to keep good teachers at your school is a definite plus for your overall educational program. If that means doing a better job of teacher induction, then do whatever it takes to improve your mentor program or to improve the quality of life for new teachers.

STRATEGY #32

Improve parental involvement in school.

"Throughout the past couple of decades, the issue of parental involvement in schools has become increasingly popular. Currently the political right and left are outspoken proponents of more parental involvement within schools" (Ramirez, 2001).

Parents must be involved in the academic process. Oftentimes parents are very concerned about sports and various other extracurricular activities but don't place much emphasis on academics. Part of the process of improving academic performance is convincing parents of the importance of being involved with their child's schoolwork. We do not live in a society where the father works during the day and the mother stays home to raise the children anymore. There are many different, nontraditional family situations these days, such as single-parent families and families with both parents working. As a result, it is more important than ever for schools to make a serious effort to enlist the help of parents in the academic process. One of the keys to any program of academic improvement is parental involvement. Research in the 1990s has linked parental involvement to increased student performance (Epstein, 1995; Flaxman and Inger, 1992; Hickman, Greenwood, and Miller, 1995; Lee, 1994).

Techniques to promote parental involvement include issuing standardized progress reports or formal report cards every four-and-a-half weeks and making phone calls to parents of problem children. Some principals require that teachers call parents a specified number of times per year. This is an excellent idea.

These methods are often the minimum requirements for most schools. Principals need to have additional plans to increase parental involvement in their schools. First of all, get the parents to come to school as much as possible. You want to show off your strengths and show that the weaknesses are not as bad as people think. Have an Open House night every semester; set up a parent resource center at your school and make sure it gets publicized; purchase an automated phone system to call parents at night if their child is absent or has a problem at school (remember that the automated system should never replace personal calls, but is just another contact tool); and provide parenting skills workshops at night. I have seen some school districts bring outstanding motivational speakers in to promote parental involvement and the district's parental training programs with good results. There are a lot of publishers that produce literature for parents, but I have also seen districts produce high-quality materials themselves. *The key is to have parents involved in the academic process as much as possible.*

SUGGESTED ACTIVITIES FOR CHAPTER 3

1. Bring sample lesson plans to class to be used in class discussion. Have the class design a lesson plan form.

2. Critique two current articles from professional journals mentioned in this chapter.

3. Prepare a class presentation on a school reform model.

4. Be prepared to discuss how your school handles first-year teachers.

5. Prepare a staff development lesson to be presented to the class.

6. Discuss how staff development is implemented in your school district.

4

COMMUNITY
RELATIONS

Our schools do not exist in a vacuum. To be successful, modern schools must be integral parts of the communities they serve. Schools cannot be separate entities with their collective head stuck in the ground, completely oblivious to the needs and concerns of the surrounding area. It is the principal's responsibility to foster strong relations with the various groups representing the local population. A principal must always be aware that the school's success is based largely on the community's perception of the school.

Eventually, schools may hire a public relations representative to handle interaction with the community, but until then the principal is responsible for this task. The principal is the major source of information about school programs and activities and is responsible for disseminating this information to the community (Wood, Nicholson, and Findley, 1985).

STRATEGY #33

Have teachers call parents.

The most important public relations tool a school district possesses is its staff. From custodians to the district superintendent, each employee is an ambassador for the school district. Having said this, the most important of these representatives are the teachers because they have the most direct contact with the students. Therefore, it is imperative that teachers communicate with parents as much as possible.

There are many ways for schools to communicate with the community. Report cards and midterm progress reports are two common methods, but written notices often do not make it into parent's hands. Thus, teachers need to make personal phone calls to parents on a regular basis. At the very least, parents should be called when a child is failing or is a discipline problem. These phone calls can help with a variety of situations. Parents often get upset when their children fail a course or get in trouble. A teacher calling the parent at the initial occurrence of the problem can help to ease the situation. As a principal you never want to hear the parent say "If someone had only called me I could have done something."

Oftentimes, however, some teachers are afraid to call parents for fear that the parent will give them a hard time. While this does happen sometimes, most parents generally appreciate the fact that someone cares enough about their children to pick up the phone and, in turn, that teacher will have a supporter for life. In cases of discipline problems, sometimes all it takes to alleviate the problem is a simple phone call. Some students are holy terrors until their parents find out. Even more important are those telephone calls just to tell parents how good their child is doing. Often we fail to do anything for those average students who don't excel but are good children and students. I require teachers to call each child's parents every grading period. This not only sets the parent at ease but is an excellent public relations tool as well.

STRATEGY #34

Publicize your school.

As previously mentioned, the school's reputation is largely based on the community's perception of the school. Today, schools in the

United States suffer from negative publicity from all sides, ranging from incidents like the Columbine shooting to students not being able to read and write. As administrators, it is our challenge to regularly promote our schools in a positive light to the public.

There are a variety of ways to get positive publicity out to the community. The following are some suggestions that should be of help in this endeavor:

1. Develop a relationship with local media people (television, print, and radio). Members of the press are quick to report a shooting at school or a gang fight. If you have developed a personal relationship with media representatives, you may be able to get them to report on your school's career day or when a teacher receives an award. Many newspapers, radio, and television have reporters on staff who are assigned to education. Find out who these people are and make use of them. Too many administrators say that the media never reports anything positive about their schools. Part of that situation is the principals' fault. Get the positive information about your school out to the media.

2. Print your own school or districtwide newsletter and send it out once or twice a month.

3. Send a calendar of school events to all parents on a monthly basis. Make sure the calendar is printed in the local newspaper also.

4. Write a guest column on an educational issue for the editorial page of the local newspaper.

5. Make promoting the school's positive image a part of your faculty evaluation process by posing the question: "What have you done as a teacher to promote the school's image or publicize your class in the community this year?"

6. Put someone in charge of creating and maintaining a website dedicated to your school. All of your school announcements can

be posted here. The website should include links to teachers' web pages, which should contain information on class assignments, projects, and so on.

7. School announcements and news can also be posted on local cable channel's channel guide pages.

8. Local radio stations will make public service announcements during peak travel times. Take advantage of this also.

Remember, the more positive images of your school you can get across to the public, the better your overall school reputation will be. Then, when something negative does happen, your reputation doesn't suffer as badly.

STRATEGY #35

Be involved in local civic organizations.

An excellent method of promoting schools is for the principal to be involved with local civic organizations. It is a good idea for the principal to be a member of at least one group and to make appearances at others. Examples of some of these organizations are the Rotary Club, the Civitans, the Optimist Club, and the Chamber of Commerce. These organizations will typically have after-dinner or after-lunch speakers. Principals can use this as a forum to promote their school or use the opportunity to bring teachers in for the same purpose.

Members of the community, especially people who don't have children, often have misconceptions about school issues. Often people can have the impression through misinformation or hearsay that schools are much worse than they actually are. If one child hears about someone having a marijuana cigarette, after it is repeated a dozen times in the community, the story is that Colombian drug dealers are ruling the halls. This is being a little facetious, but these misconceptions do happen. I once listened to a parent go on at length about the known drug dealers hanging out and making deals in the parking lot of my school. The gentleman did not realize who I was until I informed him that I was in the parking lot every day and invited him to come see how it really was. The parent took me up on my offer, saw how much better things were, and my school and I both won a valuable supporter.

Civic organization involvement is an excellent way to clear up some of these misconceptions. Through networking and personal contacts a principal can really improve the image of the school. Forming alliances with community leaders can help to publicize your mentor and adopt-a-school programs. Community leaders can also help with elections for bond issues or tax increases if you lay the proper groundwork.

STRATEGY #36

Work with parent organizations.

Parent organizations are another tool that can be used to improve the school's image and gain support for your school. If your school does not have parent support groups, meet with your coaches and activity sponsors and start some. Band parents, soccer moms, and various booster club groups can be your biggest school supporters. If you already have parent support groups, make it a point to go to some of their meetings and functions. Parents who actively support their children's extracurricular activities appreciate the fact that administrators show support for their efforts and those of their children.

This is not to say that these groups may not cause problems for principals. These groups are often narrowly focused on what is good for their particular group. The band may want new uniforms while the football team wants something else and the budget cannot compensate both. However, if the parents know that you support both groups, it will make these conflicts easier to deal with. Also, these groups can sometimes get the idea that they should control certain things, like who will be the next band director. Just remember that you are the principal. You need to let these groups know that you welcome the input, but the final decision is yours. Don't let these groups dictate to you; it is still your school to run.

STRATEGY #37

Maintain good relations with local religious leaders.

Regardless of your personal beliefs, it is usually a good idea to develop a working relationship with the religious leaders of the churches that your students attend. These people can be of help to a school in certain crisis situations. For example, when a student dies during the school year, it doesn't matter if it was an illness or some type of accident, students are going to be extremely upset and will need all the support they can get. Sometimes this is the first time students have had to deal with their own mortality. The best thing for students to do in this situation is just to let the grief out, and the more counselors you have available at these times the better. Religious leaders can be an asset to the school in crisis situations.

Finally, good relationships with community religious leaders means good relationships with the community. A religious leader's positive opinion of you and your school is invaluable and can only help create positive publicity for your school.

SUGGESTED ACTIVITIES FOR CHAPTER 4

1. Share how your district handles public relations. Is there a district-level administrator assigned to this task, or is it even dealt with on the district level?

2. Compile a list of ideas for promoting schools.

3. Discuss other means of incorporating technology into a school's community relations effort.

4. Describe how you as an administrator or prospective administrator have been involved with parent organizations.

5. Describe how you would be or have been involved with civic organizations as principal. Make a list of civic organizations in you area.

6. Research two recent articles in educational journals on school and community relations.

7. Have students prepare a presentation on school and community relations using some form of technology (PowerPoint, digital photos, etc.).

5

DISCIPLINE AND SCHOOL SAFETY

In an ideal world, a principal would come to school with nothing to do but work on improving the academic achievement of the school's students. That is a major part of a principal's responsibilities, and with new accountability standards being mandated in many states, academic achievement receives a great deal of attention. However, for quality learning to take place, there must first be a safe and orderly environment for all the students. A safe and orderly environment is the principal's responsibility.

Discipline

Historically, the aim of school discipline was to control behavior of students through the use of force. In recent decades, the control of behavior, either through privilege suspension or physical force, has been changed somewhat by the concept of self-direction (Funtwengler and Konnert, 1982).

Research over the years shows that students should be taught by the schools to develop their own concepts of right and wrong behavior (Glasser, 1969; Kohlberg, 1970; Piaget, 1932). This runs parallel with teachers, administrators, parents, communities, and politicians calling for the teaching of morals, values, and character education in today's public schools. This is not a new idea but a return to the ideas of the founding fathers of this country:

> When public education was established in America, our founding fathers agreed that responsible citizenship was to be a primary goal. This was reflected in Thomas Jefferson's philosophy that democracy could be protected only by establishing a nation of independently minded self-governing learners—learners who understood that virtuous behavior is critical for democracy's survival. Schools were to imbue students with a moral sense of developing reasoning linked to just and caring behavior. Radically different from the practices of other nations at that time, religion was to play no direct role in this mission and the role of the federal government, if any, would be minimal. For sure "habits of virtue" were directly taught at home, at church, and in the community, as well as in the school. (Bear, 1998, p. 14)

The school's role has become increasingly important in today's society precisely because the "habits of virtue," in many cases, are not being taught at home or in the community. The public and educators tend to blame each other for the problems of society. The public believes that schools should be teaching students to be responsible citizens, that values and discipline should be taught by the schools, and that schools are not handling discipline problems well (Elam, Rose, and Gallup, 1996). Educators believe that the lack of student preparedness to learn, lack of positive parental involvement, poverty, and student apathy are the major problems that they face today (U.S. Department of Education, 1996).

Having said all of this, discipline is still ultimately the responsibility of the individual school principal. The strategies outlined in this chapter will help principals deal with their discipline responsibilities.

School Safety

One of the hottest discipline topics in the United States today is that of school security and safety. It is a topic that concerns not only school administration and local school boards but also teachers, students, parents, and entire communities. State legislatures, the U.S. Congress, major federal agencies such as the Department of Justice, and the President are concerned about the safety of our school children. Why is school safety such a hot topic today? That question is not hard to answer. Everyone in the country is aware of the gruesome list of school shootings that have occurred in the past few years: Pearl High School in Mississippi; Paducah, Kentucky; Jonesboro, Arkansas; and Columbine High School in Colorado. As a building principal in a small town, I have seen firsthand the hysteria that these events have caused. I didn't work on anything else for weeks after the Columbine incident. Guns and violence have been a part of school life for some time.

Violent incidents have become widespread in our schools:

> During the 1996–1997 school year, about 21% of all public high schools and 19% of all public middle schools reported at least one serious violent crime to the police or law enforcement representatives. Four percent of all public elementary schools did the same. One third of schools with enrollment of 1000 or more students reported at least one serious violent crime. (U.S. Department of Education, 1998, p. 10)

Even after citing these statistics, "the vast majority of America's schools are safe places" (U.S. Department of Education, 1998, p. 5). It is the principal's responsibility to see that our nation's schools stay safe. Safety ranks with academic achievement as a top priority for administrators. The following strategies should be helpful to administrators as they deal with problems of discipline and school safety in their individual schools.

STRATEGY #38

Be fair and consistent with every discipline decision that you make.

Being fair and consistent each time you make a discipline decision is one of the keys to being a successful school administrator. This is also one of the most difficult aspects of being a principal because each discipline problem is unique in it's own way. Good principals should strive to make similar decisions in similar situations. Individual students or groups of students should be treated equally; blacks should not be treated differently than whites and Asians should not be treated differently than Hispanics. Similarly, the child of the president of the school board should not be treated differently than any other child in that school. If you truly are a prejudiced person, you need to find another line of work.

Prejudice has no place in the public school where we teach all of the children that come through our doors and treat them all the same. Treating students equally is easier to achieve in theory than in practice. Oftentimes, pressure is applied by outside forces to bias the principal's decision. If a principal succumbs to this pressure, his or her reputation is ruined. However, if the principal constantly makes similar decisions in similar situations, his or her credibility in the community and professional life will be greatly improved. People will see that you are always trying to do what is right for the students and your school. Everyone won't always agree with each of your decisions, but they will respect those decisions because they are sound.

Principals get into trouble when they give someone special treatment, and it doesn't take long for the students and the community to realize it if one group is being favored over another. Favoritism can only hurt a principal's reputation in the community. I'm sure everyone has heard the expressions "that's politics," "it's who you know," or "it's whoever has the most pull." Try to keep this from being true about you and your school. Favoring one group at the expense of another can be rewarding in the short term but will inevitably prove to be extremely damaging to the principal and the school.

STRATEGY #39

Have a schoolwide discipline plan.

"School must be a safe and protected environment, where a student can come to learn without fear" (Wong and Wong, 1998, p. 151). Every school in the country has some type of discipline plan, and they all work with varying degrees of success. Principals need to take a look at the plan in place at their school to see if there is anything that you want to delete. A good rule to follow is not to have anything in the plan that you cannot reasonably justify or explain to anyone that questions it. You don't have to scrap your present plan. If it is working well, keep it or just modify parts of it.

If you want to totally redo your discipline plan, there are some good plans readily available by asking nearby school districts to send you copies of their discipline plans or refer to Harry Wong's *The First Days of School*, in which an entire chapter is devoted to discipline plans ("How to have an effective discipline plan"). You might also want to look at Lee Canter's materials on assertive discipline. Keep in mind, however, that teachers believe assertive discipline means that principals are supposed to be assertive while principals believe that teachers are the ones who need to be taking care of discipline in their classrooms. You will also want to look at William Glasser's work on the control theory, which deals with self-regulating and self-governing behavior. The community building approach to discipline, as described by Haim Ginott, Jacob Kounin, and Alfie Kohn, should also be considered. Take a look at these different approaches to discipline and classroom management and adapt whatever you can use to your own school plan.

As a response to the increased occurrence of some discipline problems, many schools and districts have adopted zero-tolerance policies for such things as possession of drugs or possession of a weapon. Be careful of these zero-tolerance plans because while zero tolerance should be a goal in any school, any plan that calls for automatic suspension or expulsion can cause you problems. You want to be fair and consistent, but you don't want to be backed into a corner by your plan. Dewayne Wickham of Gannet News Service said that "zero tolerance shouldn't mean no common sense. Public school zero-tolerance policies are bad law. They are an overreaction to the highly publicized spate of crimes committed by a handful of students around the nation" (2001). Wickham was talking about a student who was suspended for taking a knife away from a student who was contemplating suicide.

We, as educators, are supposed to focus on teaching students, not putting them out on the streets. Weapons are a good example. A student drives to school with a shotgun in a gun rack in the back window of his truck. A school district's zero-tolerance policy and state law says that the student is to be expelled for one calendar year for having a weapon on campus. The student claims he forgot it was there. The date is October 15. If the student is expelled, the student will lose credit for the fall semester, the spring semester, and the following fall semester. This could effectively ruin a child's chances for graduating. Someone that brought a gun, with intentions of using it, would just have to face the consequences. What do you do about this situation? Do you expel a child for drinking a beer in the parking lot after a football game? If you have a zero tolerance for drugs policy you might. These are the kinds of things you need to think about before you write a zero-tolerance policy.

STRATEGY #40

Go to the 4 × 4 block schedule.

If your school is following a traditional six- or seven-period school day schedule, you seriously need to look at changing to the 4 × 4 block schedule to help decrease your discipline problems. "In the 4 × 4 semester plan, or accelerated schedule as it is called in a few states, students enroll in four classes that meet for about 90 minutes every day for 90 days. Teachers teach three courses each semester. Year-long courses are completed in one semester. Students enroll in four new courses (teachers teach three) in the second semester" (Canady and Rettig 1992, p. 14).

One major advantage to block scheduling is a significant decrease in the amount of discipline problems and office referrals that are reported by schools implementing some form of the block schedule (Buckman, King, and Ryan, 1995; Carroll, 1987; O'Neil, 1995). Having fewer discipline problems allows principals and assistant principals to take on different roles as the amount of time taken in dealing with discipline problems is reduced. An overall school climate that fosters discipline is necessary for learning to take place. A school district must, first and foremost, have good discipline in order to have a school climate conducive to learning. Many school districts lose sight of that very important fact. The block schedule can be an important tool to facilitate good discipline and foster an overall atmosphere where learning takes place, which should be the number one goal of every school district in the country. Researchers at the University of North Carolina at Charlotte say that:

Schools that have adopted block schedules report a significant reduction in absenteeism and drastic reductions in discipline problems. Discipline will continue to be problem for beginning teachers and for some individuals on any staff, and a detailed training program should be a required part of the transition to block scheduling. However, students generally like the opportunities provided by the block schedule, and the varied teaching methods hold their attention. The students like the schedule because it works for them, and so they create fewer discipline problems. Moreover, they attend classes more frequently because cutting means missing a more substantial portion of the subject matter of a course. (Queen and Gaskey, 1997, p. 161)

On a traditional school day schedule, students move from classroom to classroom from five to seven times a day. This means that the students have five to seven different teachers, different textbooks, different teaching styles, and different discipline styles. "Releasing thousands of students into narrow hallways, six or seven times each day for four or five minutes to go to the restroom or to their lockers create noise, stress and in many schools, bedlam" (Daves, 1998, p. 21). To say that constant classroom rotation leads to disjointed and disconnected learning and discipline is an understatement. Numerous changes also limit students' activities that develop higher-level thinking and problem-solving skills. For example, science teachers have always wanted more time for their laboratory projects. Teaching 150 students also limits individual attention to students (Khazzaka, 1997).

Research in Lybbert suggests that when the block schedule is implemented from a building-level principal's perspective, discipline problems decrease. The decrease in discipline problems because of fewer class changes is definitely a very large benefit of this scheduling system:

When you reduce the number of passing periods, you reduce the number of number of opportunities for disruption in the hallway. Principals try to make a practice of standing in the halls and having teachers stand in the hall during passing periods because of the need to supervise students moving about in close quarters. Most fights at school occur when there is a lack of direct supervision, such as before and after school, passing periods, and during lunch. Tardies will also be reduced for the same reason; students have fewer classes to be tardy. The real benefits in terms of school discipline, however, seem to be related to changing the overall school environment. It should not be surprising when both students and teachers report they are happier in a blocked schedule that disciplinary problems decline. The fact that students do better in their classes also affects attendance, failure rates, and other factors that are known to be associated with students who are continuously in trouble at school. As students experience more engagement and success at school, their discipline problems decline drastically. (1998, pp. 14–15)

According to a National Association of Secondary School Principals (NASSP) study conducted in the early 1980s in California, the major incidents of misconduct were "tardiness; fighting; disrespect for teachers; disruptive school behavior; personal rivalries; extortion; theft; cutting class; racial tensions; and unprovoked assaults" (Reed, 1983). The very obvious benefit of block scheduling is alleviating some of these major problems simply by reducing the number of class changes. The fewer class changes there are:

- the fewer tardies a school has

- the fewer opportunities there are to cut class or leave campus

- the fewer opportunities there are for students to fight between classes

- the fewer opportunities there are for large groups of students to congregate and disrupt the school process

A study done at an Indiana high school found that:

Within the first week of the block schedule, the hallways were quieter during passing periods. In fact, the school did not have a single hallway fight the whole first semester, a never-before recorded statistic. Not only did the students seem in less of a hurry (the five-minute passing period remained the same), but students were in the hallway half as many times with the 4-block schedule. There was more time in class to settle conflicts. Because of these improvements, fewer students were assigned to in-school supervision. (Snyder, 1997, p. 7)

One Texas high school with a population of 2,000 students claimed only one discipline referral in a seven-day period (Lybbert, 1998). That kind of result is not considered typical, but a 25% to 35% decrease in discipline problems is common. In fact, a study of a Wisconsin high school showed these results almost exactly, with a 23% decline in office referrals (Fitzpatrick and Moyers, 1997). Some research shows an even higher decline in discipline problems. One middle school reported their total number of office referrals decreased by 57.9%. In this same middle school, in-school suspension rates decreased by 60.1% (Hackman, 1995).

Research in Snow (2001) provides results from a study of how teachers, administrators, and students perceived the difference in occurrences of discipline problems on the block schedule as opposed to the traditional six- or seven-period schedule. The following conclusions were drawn from this study:

1. Teachers did believe that there is a difference in occurrence of discipline problems on the block schedule as opposed to the traditional schedule. In particular, teachers felt that there was a higher occurrence of discipline problems such as stealing, fighting, throwing things on campus, and drugs on the traditional six- or seven-period day schedule. The only problem that was thought to occur more on the block schedule was excessive talking in the classroom.

2. Administrators also believed that there is a higher occurrence of discipline problems on the six- or seven-period day schedule. However, administrators thought that all of the discipline problems included in the study occurred at a higher rate on the traditional schedule.

3. The data indicated that a large percentage of administrators felt strongly that the block schedule reduces discipline problems. Percentages were smaller for teachers and smaller still for students.

4. Analysis of the data indicated that over 80% of the administrators surveyed in this study thought that the block schedule results in safer, more secure school grounds.

5. The vast majority of administrators surveyed thought that the block schedule results in a more orderly school climate.

6. The majority of teachers, administrators, and students did not want to return to the traditional six- or seven-period schedule because of better discipline on the block schedule.

In summary, this study found that there was a difference in how administrators, teachers, and students perceive the occurrence of discipline problems on the block schedule as opposed to the six- or seven-period day. Administrators felt that there are fewer discipline problems on the block schedule. Teachers agreed that there are less discipline problems on the block schedule but thought the difference was not as large as the administrator's believed it to be. Students did not believe that there is a difference in the occurrence of discipline problems from one schedule to the next, but this could have been a result of their general apathy toward the survey itself. Finally, none of the groups wanted to return to the six- or seven-period day if discipline was the deciding factor. *Principals, if you want fewer discipline problems go to the block schedule.*

STRATEGY #41

Make your teachers discipline their students.

Making teachers discipline their students can be one of the most important things that a principal does. Principals tend to be take-charge, assertive types of people. If a teacher brings a principal a problem, it will usually be taken care of quickly because principals tend to jump all over problems when they appear. Teachers know this and will take advantage of it. If you are not careful, teachers will have the principal or assistant principal doing all their discipline.

Classroom discipline is the teacher's responsibility, and principals must ensure that teachers take care of the discipline in their classroom. A teacher that constantly sends students to the office is not getting the job done. Principals can tell who the weak teachers are by the number of discipline referrals they have. As principal, it is your job to provide direction and professional development in classroom management to weak teachers so that countless students aren't sent to the office, causing disruption to the educational process.

The following is an example of what I am talking about. A teacher gets up in a faculty meeting and says, "the use of profanity on this campus is out of control." What the teacher wants is for the administration to take care of this. As I just said, a principal's first reaction to something like this is "By God, I'll take care of this." The right way to handle this is to ask the teacher, "What do you do when you hear profanity." Administrators can't deal with things if they are not brought to their attention. What the teacher wants to hear is that the principal will take care of it. Teachers need to know that the administration will take care of discipline, but at the same time, they need to do their part also.

In a typical high school of 600 to 1,000 students, there will be one principal and one or two assistant principals. There is no way that two or three people can discipline all of these students. It takes a cooperative effort of all school personnel to keep this many students in line, which is why it is so important that teachers handle their own classroom discipline.

Another part of this is making sure that teachers help out on campus by being at their duty posts. A little time spent on supervision of teachers can go a long way to help a principal maintain a safe and orderly school climate. Principals cannot be everywhere at once and should not be required to do so. Principals are more likely to face burnout, seek early retirement, or leave the profession if they don't make their teachers handle their own discipline problems. When a student is sent to the office for things like class disruption or talking, my first comment is going to be directed at the teacher. "What have you done to correct this situation?" If the answer is "nothing," I will tell the teacher to take some sort of action first before sending them to the office. Call the parents. Assign a detention. The teacher should attempt to deal with the problem first. Only then will I get involved if behavior doesn't improve.

It is important to note that once a problem is sent to the principal, the principal needs to handle it. What I mean here is that the teacher should not tell the principal what action to take. I have had teachers send students to the office with a note saying what punishment should occur. No; as principal, you will decide what punishment, if any, will take place. By sending the child to the principal, the teacher has already said that he or she could not handle the situation, making it the principal's responsibility, not the teacher's. Some teachers would have students shot for chewing gum. The principal is the one who has to live with the decision, so make sure it is a decision you are comfortable with. *Make your teachers discipline. It will simplify your job.*

STRATEGY #42

Call parents about discipline problems.

In Strategy #38, I talked about how the principal and assistant principal could not do all the discipline in a school and needed help from their faculty. Principals also need to enlist the help of parents in disciplining their children. The best way to do this is by contacting parents by telephone as soon as possible when there is a discipline problem. I believe many teachers and some administrators are reluctant—or even afraid—to contact parents when their children are causing problems at school. I'm not quite sure why many educators don't want to contact parents. I do know, however, that quality teachers are constantly in contact with parents. It could be that teachers are either afraid of irate parents or are not confident in their ability to deal with parents or teachers may even avoid parents because the teachers cannot justify their actions toward students. Sure you will have some unpleasant experiences with parents, but, for the most part, a simple phone call will make that parent your supporter for life because parents appreciate it when they feel someone cares about their child. Sometimes a phone call can make the problem disappear completely because many children act out when they think their parents won't find out but sing a different tune when mom and dad find out. Make a call and see how fast some problems can be solved.

There are other means of communication with parents. Many schools mail a written notice to the parents of each student who has some type of discipline problem. Other schools have automated calling machines that call a student's home after school hours to inform the parents of the discipline problems. These methods aren't as effective as personal calls because they can easily be circumvented by the students who learn to answer the phone at night and be the first one to get the mail. But they are alternatives and can serve as documentation (see Strategy #41, "Make your teachers discipline their students").

The main thing that you want to avoid is to have an ongoing problem escalate until a child gets into serious trouble. Once this happens and you take serious action against a student such as suspension or expulsion, it is much easier to explain and justify if you have been in contact with the parent all along. The last thing you want to hear from a parent is "No one ever told me." You have got to be able to show that efforts were made to inform the parent of their child's discipline problem.

STRATEGY #43

Document your discipline problems.

We live in a very litigious society, making it wise for principals to always keep written records of all discipline situations. Before the widespread use of computers in schools, principals kept a paper file on each student that included a written report of each discipline problem with that child. Today all schools have computers with specific software programs to help administrators keep track of disciplinary actions. Principals can enter the data themselves or a secretary or data technician can be designated to do this. However, it is still wise to keep a paper copy in case data is lost. Also, make sure that data is not lost or deleted from year to year.

Another reason to keep good documentation is that it makes it easier to deal with students who are a constant problem. The principal's handling of children with chronic discipline problems is very important to how that principal is perceived. It is much easier to expel or place a child in an alternative school if you have documentation of all of that student's discipline referrals. Good documentation also makes it easier to deal with the parents of the student. Most schools have some sort of appeal process in discipline actions, such as a review committee or the school board. If you have to go through an appeal, you had better have your documentation or you could really look unprofessional at the least and incompetent at the worst. The same thing applies to court cases. *If you want to be successful and survive as a principal, document all your disciplinary actions.*

STRATEGY #44

Don't make discipline policies that
you aren't going to enforce.

Principals should always be aware of the public's perception of the school. Discipline in schools is important to the average person in the community, and everyone has personal experience with schools to use as a measure of what they think good discipline should be. At the same time, most people have some connection to the local school through their children or the children of friends or relatives. In some towns, the school can even be one of the largest employers in the community, making it the citizen's central focus.

A school's standard of behavior and discipline can be poorly perceived in the community if it appears that certain rules are not enforced. If you aren't going to enforce a policy, don't put it in your handbook. Not enforcing policies makes the administration look weak and ineffective and could also be grounds for dismissal. When a new principal takes over a school, there may be discipline policies that do not coincide with that principal's philosophy of discipline but these policies must still be enforced. If it is in the student handbook, it needs to be enforced. The handbook can be changed if there is a policy that you do not agree with, but that must be done through proper channels and procedures.

To have an effective discipline program at a school, it is extremely important that all teachers enforce the rules equally. If one teacher enforces a rule and other teachers do not, it can only lead to problems. For example, some schools have a rule that students are not allowed to wear caps at school. If teachers do not see this as a problem or a class disruption, take the rule out of the handbook. One of the things that you learn as an administrator is not to spend a lot of time and energy fighting battles that do not mean much. However, if you leave the rule about caps in your student handbook and some people do not enforce it, it can only lead to problems for the school. Teachers who do not enforce the rule are seen to be lax on discipline while teachers who do enforce the rule are seen as unreasonable. Students notice these inconsistencies and start to believe that they can get away with other things or refuse to do as they are told because not everyone enforces the rule, which leads to an escalation of the problem. This all seems to be much ado about nothing, but ignoring the smallest rule can cause problems. *If, as a school, a rule is not going to be enforced, get rid of it.*

STRATEGY #45

Remove graffiti from the school immediately.

As previously mentioned, one of the major responsibilities of a principal is to provide a safe and orderly environment for all of the children at a school. As a part of this, there is no place for graffiti or vandalism at a well-run school. The principal needs to have a person, usually the custodian, who is responsible for seeing that graffiti is either removed or painted over on a daily basis. For some reason—probably because students are not always under observation in this area—students often put graffiti on restroom walls. If schools use plastic partitions, they can be easily cleaned and even heated and reshaped to remove carving and other graffiti (Kennedy, 2001).

Graffiti can cover a broad range of topics. Some graffiti is gang related and can cause trouble between rival gangs at school. Administrators need to take note of gang-related graffiti and inform law enforcement officials. Graffiti can also take the form of racial slurs or other derogatory statements, such as sexual remarks directed toward students and teachers, that can also cause unrest within the school. It is extremely important that this type of graffiti be removed as quickly as possible as your teachers and students certainly deserve to be protected from this sort of thing. The standard I have always followed is that I would not want my child or spouse to be subjected to this sort of graffiti, therefore no one else should be. Principals must designate in the student handbook the consequences for students who use graffiti to promote gangs or racial slurs.

As mentioned earlier, you need to have a plan in place to see that graffiti is removed in a timely manner and then check on it constantly. All school personnel should be constantly on the lookout for this derogatory material.

STRATEGY #46

Have a crisis management plan in place.

Every school in the United States needs to have a crisis management plan in place before the start of every school year. Not only do schools need to be prepared for natural disasters, but it has also recently become clear that educators must be prepared for manmade crisis situations as well. School administrators need to keep tragedies, such as the shootings at Pearl and Columbine high schools, constantly in their thoughts in order to identify these conflicts before they happen. The following are some of the items to be included in a comprehensive crisis management plan:

1. Evacuation plan for fire drills and bomb threats

2. Hazardous materials spill evacuation plan

3. Plan for intruders on campus

4. Plan for coping with traumatic events

5. Tornado plan

6. Severe weather security plan

Every school in the country should have a plan for fire evacuation. Local fire departments stage these drills at schools on a regular basis.

This same evacuation plan can be used for dealing with bomb threats; however, there needs to be coordination with local law enforcement as to how the school will be searched. If the students are going to remain outside for extended periods of time, plans need to be made for shelter and rest room facilities. As an assistant principal, I worked at a school that had sixteen bomb threats in one year. The school staff became very adept at evacuations, but the students' entire learning process was greatly disrupted. This particular rash of threats did not stop until the responsible parties were arrested.

If your school is near railroad tracks or a major highway, there should be a plan in place to evacuate students to another location in case of a hazardous materials spill. This sort of accident may require loading students on buses or cordoning off streets to allow students to walk to another location. Students and faculty need to be drilled on these procedures several times a year. Again, this requires coordination with local law enforcement.

In these unsettled times, it is also important to have a plan in place for intruders on campus. In recent years, there have been several occasions on which students have brought weapons to school for the purpose of shooting faculty and staff. Now we must also be aware of terrorist threats or estranged parents or spouses attempting to kidnap or harm their children or ex-spouse. Principals need to be able to communicate these crises quickly with teachers and staff by using a process, such as a simple code word broadcast on the intercom to alert teachers to lock their doors and keep the students away from doors and windows. This is also something that needs to be reviewed often with faculty, so that they will react immediately when the code is announced.

Another area that needs to be addressed is a plan for dealing with traumatic events that can affect your student body. What does your school do when a student is killed in an automobile accident? What do you do when a student commits suicide? These are the type of contingencies that you need to be prepared for. In larger schools, this type of occurrence may not affect as many students as it would in a smaller, more close-knit school. Either way, you are going to have students searching for a way to deal with there feelings caused by this traumatic event. It has been my experience that it is best to just let the students get everything out of their systems. To do this, a school needs to have plenty of extra counseling, such as local religious leaders and mental health workers, available. Your community will appreciate you and your staff handling their children with care and concern during these times. Realize that this event is going to disrupt your school, and be prepared to deal with it.

School administrators also need to have plans in effect for severe weather emergencies, such as tornadoes, hurricanes, or snow-storms. Weather systems vary in different parts of the country and the staff and students should be trained to deal with whatever situation is common in their school's area. These procedures should be practiced until everyone in a school knows where to go automatically. All of these plans should also include methods for student and parent notification of closings and procedures for early dismissal of students. Additionally, these plans should illustrate the method for securing equipment, such as computers, before schools are closed due to weather.

If your school district does not have a comprehensive crisis management plan, developing a good one should be a top priority.

STRATEGY #47

Have your school evaluated for safety.

If your school has not been for evaluated for security and safety, have this done as soon as possible. Your local law enforcement agencies will be glad to help you with this. The closest FBI office will send an agent to help evaluate your school if asked to do so. Some states have checklists for school facility safety available that you can use yourself. For example, the Virginia Department of Education has developed a "Checklist for the Safety and Security of Buildings and Grounds" to be used on an annual basis by every school in Virginia. The Virginia checklist contains eighty-four items that are divided into three categories: school exterior and play area, school interior, and miscellaneous.

Examples of school exterior questions are as follows. Are signs posted for visitors to report to the office? Are shrubs and foliage trimmed to allow clear lines of sight? Is access restricted to bus loading and unloading areas? Is there adequate lighting around the exterior of the building?

School interior questions focus on other areas. Are unused classrooms locked? Are students restricted from unused classrooms? Is there an alarm system? Is that alarm system checked on a regular basis?

The miscellaneous section has numerous questions about maintenance responsibilities. Is there a schedule for maintenance to check lights, locks, and outlying buildings? Are mechanical rooms locked and hazardous storage areas locked?

Even if you use one of these checklists, it is still a good idea to contact local law enforcement so that you are included in their plans for dealing with security incidents at your school. Once your school has been evaluated, follow as many of the safety recommendations as your community and budget will allow. Strategies #47, #48, and #49 discuss several measures that can be taken to improve safety in schools. Other suggested measures include the following:

- installing security cameras
- installing metal detectors at all entrances
- hiring security guards
- having teachers patrol hallways and restrooms as part of there assigned duties

Security cameras are useful as a deterrent to incidents of damage to school property and incidents of school violence that can take place in the areas being monitored by these cameras. Also, the tapes are a record that can be used as evidence against perpetrators of these acts. I was once able to identify some of my students committing an act of vandalism against a school in another district from a surveillance tape, which resulted in their apprehension and punishment.

Metal detectors, of course, are helpful in keeping guns and explosive devices from being brought into a school. To properly implement a metal detector system, however, the school must limit access to a few entrances and hire or designate security personnel to run the equipment. The additional cost for this equipment and staff could be prohibitive for some schools. Also, not all communities are ready to see metal detectors and security guards at every school entrance, but this may be changing in light of all the recent school shootings and terrorist incidents.

Personally, I am in favor of having security guards walking the hallways and patrolling the parking lots of our school. The key is to find personnel who are well suited to working with young people. The advantages for principals are tremendous. Security guards can help to break up serious fights, patrol halls, look for suspicious substances, help with irate parents, escort students off campus, and look for unauthorized entrance or leaving of the campus. Principals can use this kind of help.

Having teachers patrol hallways and restrooms during their planning period is an option, but it does have its drawbacks. Teachers do not like additional nonteaching duties, and accreditation requirements often entail that their planning periods be free of other duties. So, be careful using teachers during this time, even though making teachers responsible for helping with security and discipline is usually a good thing, as illustrated in Strategy #18.

STRATEGY #48

Enclose your school as much as possible.

One of the most effective ways to ensure the overall safety of a school's grounds is to enclose the entire complex with a chain link fence topped with razor wire. Is this feasible? No, most communities would be up in arms over something like that. However, steps can be taken to allow for a more secure campus and grounds, without making the school look like a prison camp. There are a variety of ways to approach this without throwing up a fence around the school. One approach is to seal all but a few entrances that can be more easily monitored. Walls sealing off the spaces between buildings can be installed and recessed so they are not as visible.

What will enclosing the school do for your school? Since it is unwise to let people walk onto our campus without our knowledge, access to the school grounds must be limited. Principals have to be worried about terrorists, parents trying to kidnap children, child molesters, and other assorted crazies coming onto campus. Anything you can do to limit access is a plus.

STRATEGY #49

Consider school uniforms.

The current literature is very much in favor of increased parental involvement and institution of a dress code in today's schools. Stanley (1996) explains some of the benefits:

> School uniforms are one of several strategies being used by this nation's public schools to restore order in the classroom and safety in the school. Recently, it seems as if everyone—from the president to the national media to the local PTA—is talking about the utility of this approach. Why

school uniforms? Principals believe that the use of school uniforms can have a positive effect on violence reduction and academic achievement, and can reduce the need for discipline. . . . Popular press articles report that school uniforms control violence associated with attending school . . ., improve attendance rates . . ., modify behavior . . ., improve academic achievement . . ., reduce the focus on fashion contests . . ., and promote ideas and achievement.

Uniforms are getting the most attention at middle and high schools, where security and school unity are big issues, along with the controversial extremes of current teen fashion, such as spaghetti-strap tanks, face painting, and body piercing. "You'd be amazed at the amount of time administrators have been spending on what kids are wearing to school," says Susan Galletti, a middle-school specialist at the National Association of Secondary School Principals. "With uniforms, all that is eliminated, and they can spend more time on teaching and learning" (Wingert, 1999).

I was not in favor of school uniforms for public schools until I actually worked at a school with a standard uniform. One of the main advantages is that administrators and teachers can immediately tell if someone is on campus who does not belong. This is an immense help in keeping the campus safe.

Selecting a standard school uniform is relatively easy. Khaki pants and a white or light blue shirt with an optional school logo are always good. Students and parents both seem to like the idea of uniforms. Students say it is just easier and less trouble to dress for school while parents like it because it is less expensive.

A standard uniform will not solve all of a principal's dress code problems because there will always be students who will challenge the code. But on the whole it will make things a lot easier. Additionally, there is legal backing in some states for uniforms at public schools. The Fifth Circuit Court of Appeals upheld the 1999 mandatory school uniform policy for Louisiana's Bossier Parish public schools. The Bossier Parish school board adopted the policy for the 1999–2000 school year for the purpose of reducing disciplinary problems and met with tremendous opposition. The court said it was not their responsibility to decide the best way to educate the country's young people (Simpson, 2001).

STRATEGY #50

Consider school ID badges for students and teachers.

Another unobtrusive way to increase security is to institute an identification badge system. A sign of a good principal is the ability to tell at a glance who is or who is not a student at your school. Principals can instinctively tell immediately if someone looks like they do not belong. However, with all of the trouble that has found its way onto school campuses these days, it is necessary for everyone involved with a school to be able to identify nonstudents on campus.

Principals, teachers, staff, and students all need to recognize who does or does not belong. Many schools have started requiring their students to wear identification badges at all times. Pictures can be taken by a digital camera, stored on a computer disk, and printed in a matter of minutes (Partington, 1999). These cards can also be used to purchase meals in the cafeteria and check out books from the library. These new cards have an additional added benefit in that "students who qualify for free or reduced-cost lunches now apply for them, because using the card, they are not identified and stigmatized when they get to the cashier in the cafeteria line" ("Increase security," 1992, p. 19).

STRATEGY #51

Be prepared to deal with a student with a weapon.

There will come a time where a principal will be called to deal with a student who has a weapon of some type. Principals need to have a plan for this type of situation. Do not do what I did the first time I received a report from a teacher that a student had a gun in his back pocket. I ran to the classroom, called the student outside, and said, "Show me what you have in your pocket." I realized as the student started to pull something from his pocket that I had made probably the biggest mistake of my life. I was extremely lucky that the student only had a loaded magazine from a nine-millimeter pistol and not the actual gun. If the student had actually had a loaded pistol, myself, the teacher, or the children in the classroom could have been in mortal danger because I did not properly handle the situation. As an administrator my first responsibility was to protect the students and teacher, which is what I thought I was doing.

When you get a report of a weapon at school, call the police immediately. If possible, wait until the police arrive to confront the student. Remove the student from the classroom as quickly as possible to lessen the danger to others. If you have a security guard on campus, get the guard to help you remove the student. As soon as you get the student outside the classroom, find out if the student does in fact have a weapon and take it from the student. As a school administrator, I do not advocate strip searches. However, you can usually determine if a student is carrying a gun or knife by having them empty out their pockets. If you still suspect a weapon is being concealed, wait until the police get there before taking further action. Always make sure that the student cannot cause you any harm as these proceedings are taking place. If this means restraining the student in some way, do it to protect yourself and others.

If a student or intruder is brandishing a weapon, call the police and initiate your lockdown procedures as outlined in your crisis management plan. If other students are in a common area, get them to safety as soon as possible. You don't have to be a hero, but if you are prepared it could make the difference in avoiding another school tragedy.

STRATEGY #52

Be prepared to deal with the search of a student.

There will be times when it is necessary to search a student for drugs, weapons, stolen property, or some other type of contraband. A principal is only required to have "reasonable suspicion" that a student is in possession of an illegal substance in order to initiate a search. This principle of law was established in the 1985 case of *New Jersey v. T.L.O.* (Reutter, 1994). Law enforcement officials are held to the much higher standard of "probable cause" in order to search, but school administrators are not.

For example, if you are told by one student that another student is carrying marijuana, that is enough reason to search that student. Personally escort the student from class to a principal's office. Observe the student at all times so that he or she doesn't try to get rid of anything. On arrival in the office, request that the student show you what is in his or her pockets. Have the student turn pockets inside out. I do not recommend doing strip searches, although these searches have been upheld by the courts, as in *Williams v. Ellington* in 1991 and *Cornfield v. Consolidated High School District* in 1993 (Reutter, 1994). If at all possible, avoid strip searches, as the potential for problems is far greater than they are worth and an adequate search can usually be conducted without going that far. If the student refuses to cooperate, call the parents in immediately. The refusal to submit to a noninvasive search like this can be grounds for expulsion or suspension, depending on school board policy.

Remember to always keep an eye on a student who is suspected of having drugs because they may try to get rid of the drug on the way to the office. If a student under suspicion has a cigarette pack, look inside, as this is a favorite place to hide a couple of marijuana "joints." Also, check inside the student's wallet or purse—another common hiding place for drugs. It is a good idea to require students to carry clear or mesh bookbags to school to make it more difficult to conceal contraband. Lockers are the property of the school and can be searched at any time, with or without the student's consent if the students are clearly notified of this at the time lockers are assigned. Again there are court cases to back this up, such as *Zamora v. Pomeroy* in 1981 and *Commonwealth v. Carey* in 1990 (Reutter, 1994). "Using dogs trained to detect contraband to sniff lockers, desks, or cars does not violate the Fourth Amendment, but allowing the dogs to sniff a student's person is constitutional only upon 'individualized reasonable suspicion'" (Reutter, 1994, p. 763).

SUGGESTED ACTIVITIES FOR CHAPTER 5

1. Prepare a position paper discussing the benefits of the block schedule.
2. Prepare a position paper discussing the disadvantages of the block schedule.
3. As a group project, prepare a sample schoolwide discipline program.
4. Develop a school security checklist.
5. Prepare a class presentation in favor of school uniforms.
6. Prepare a class presentation opposing school uniforms.
7. Develop a plan to evaluate teacher's use of discipline procedures.
8. Bring a sample discipline report form to class.
9. Bring a copy of your school's crisis management plan to class.
10. Find out how graffiti is dealt with in your school.

6

ADDITIONAL DUTIES
OF A PRINCIPAL

As this book started to come together, I realized that there were some important items that had been left out because they did not fit into one of the chapters. This chapter contains experience-based strategies that, even though they do not fit into one particular category, will help principals to be successful, personally and professionally.

STRATEGY #53

Get all requests in writing.

During the course of a normal school day, principals will talk to dozens of students, teachers, and parents. A principal's day is filled with teachers and students stopping the principal as he or she makes rounds throughout the day, people calling and coming into the office to make requests, and the superintendent of the school district asking that certain things be done. I try to keep a notebook to keep track of all of the requests that are made as the day progresses. However, I have found that the best way to handle all of these requests is to always have them submitted in writing or to use e-mail to provide a form of written backup for verbal requests. Remember, using e-mail requires that you check it periodically. It is impossible for a principal to keep track of all the requests made through memory only, so a principal must, first, write down requests as much as possible, and, second, ask for written requests as a matter of everyday practice.

STRATEGY #54

Learn as many of your students' names as possible.

In these modern times, a principal must fill many different roles. At the same time, to truly be effective as an administrator, a principal cannot lose sight of the fact that children should be the focus of everything that schools do. A mark of a good principal is how many of a school's students he or she can call by name. The larger a school is, the more difficult this can be. This may not seem important on the surface, but if a principal does not know his students it can lead to that principal being distant or out of touch with the school population. It is much more effective when supervising if you can use the students given name rather than saying "hey, you." A principal should also speak to students as much as possible. Why is that important? Dealing with students on an individual basis fosters a friendlier, warmer school environment, which is important to set the stage for learning to take place. Students also need to know that their principal is accessible to them. It just makes for a better school climate, and a better school climate leads to more learning.

STRATEGY # 55

Keep faculty meetings as short as possible.

With today's demands for improved academic performance as measured by standardized test scores, many school districts are requiring more and more staff development activities after normal school hours.

Due to these increased demands on teacher's time, it is essential that principals not conduct lengthy faculty meetings. Some principals have been known to hold faculty meetings that last for several hours every week. These lengthy meetings are uncalled for and will only antagonize the staff. Too many times principals "chase rabbits" in these meetings. In other words, principals go on at length about immaterial subjects when most of the staff would rather not stay after school at all. So, if you do hold a meeting, make sure it is important and worthwhile.

Most of the time, faculty meetings can be dispensed with and re-placed by a well-thought-out memo. However, it is important that the principal meet with the faculty periodically to remind teachers who their supervisor is. Therefore, when you do have a faculty meeting, these meetings should be carefully planned and scripted with a strict agenda, enabling teachers to get in and out of the meeting in a short amount of time. Your staff will love you for the efficiency and consideration. *Don't waste your teacher's time.*

STRATEGY #56

Don't put anything in your student handbook that you cannot justify.

The student handbook is an important document that serves as a writ-ten record of all the rules and regulations that govern students' activi-ties in school. Topics covered range from grading to discipline to the student dress code. The student handbook must be well thought out and constantly reviewed and revised as needed. Keep an administra-tor's copy on hand during the school year so that, as a problem with a rule or regulation arises, you can make a notation in the handbook and revise it at the end of the school year.

The following is an example of a rule that is difficult to justify or deal with. In an attempt to improve school attendance, many schools institute a policy that exempts students with perfect attendance from nine weeks of exams or some semester tests. That should be a simple enough rule to follow, but in practice it is a different story. What do you do about a student who is never absent from school but needs to attend his grandfather's funeral? According to the policy, the principal must tell the student and parents that attending the funeral will remove the exemption. From personal experience, that situation will cause a lot of hard feelings from parents and can really damage a principal's reputation.

For this reason, exemptions should be done away with. Exemptions might be okay for high school seniors, but that should be it. How are students going to prepare for important tests like the SAT or ACT, if they don't take tests during the regular school year? With all of the high stakes testing being conducted in schools today, we would be foolish to continue to exempt students and should instead reward perfect attendance in another way.

Another example of a questionable practice that makes it into student handbooks is double-punishing students. If a student is cheating in class, is that an academic problem or a discipline problem? If you feel it is an academic problem, then the student's grade should suffer; if it is a discipline problem, take disciplinary action. But do not do both.

The main point here is to carefully examine your handbook and remove items that don't work or are problematic in any way. The handbook can be an excellent tool to govern the student body and should be designed with your school's specific needs in mind.

STRATEGY #57

Do something to relieve stress every day.

A former school superintendent I know had a cloud mural painted on the ceiling of his office that he would set aside a time period during the day when he would hold all calls and visitors and relax and stare at to relieve stress. Personally, I think this seems a trifle extreme, but I can identify with the need. As an added note, that superintendent needed open-heart surgery and became a university professor instead of remaining a superintendent.

Being a principal is a stressful position. The stress is exacerbated by the fact that it is not a good idea for principals to have close personal relationships with staff members, making it a very lonely job. Therefore it is necessary for principals to develop friendships away from school and have leisure activities outside of school. Principals often go to their school every day, even on holidays, just to walk the halls and check to make sure there hasn't been any vandalism or broken pipes or something. Get away from the school and do other things whenever possible. It doesn't really matter what it is, but it is necessary for principals to have some type of outside interests. Shop, hunt, fish, read, play with your own children . . . it doesn't matter what, but do something. Don't be consumed by work. The other path leads to principals leaving the profession or taking early retirement.

STRATEGY #58

Don't be intimidated by lawyers.

An unfortunate aspect of our society these days is that people will sue over anything at the drop of a hat. This is a fact of life that principals have to deal with. Parents are oftentimes quick to say that they are going to contact their lawyer, and principals don't have to put up with this scare tactic. The strategy for dealing with this is not complicated. When a parent mentions their lawyer, stop the meeting right there. The proper response to the mention of a lawyer is "this meeting/conversation is over—have your attorney contact the school attorney." At that point get up and walk out or escort the parent out, depending on what office you are in. Most of the time the parent will want to continue and drop the talk about lawyers. If they don't, that is what schools have lawyers on retainer for. Don't go out of your way to antagonize people, but once people bring the lawyers into it, it becomes a legal matter and is out of your hands.

STRATEGY #59

Don't be intimidated by parents.

Strategy #59 deals with not being intimidated by parents and is an extension of Strategy #58, which dealt with not being intimidated by lawyers. Some parents lose their tempers when they think that their children have been treated unfairly, and they usually take it out on the principal.

The first step in dealing with irate parents is to try to diffuse the anger. The principal needs to make statements like "let's talk about this in a reasonable manner" or "let's talk to the teacher and get this cleared up." One important ground rule is that parents should not be allowed to use profanity toward the principal, the teacher, or anyone else in your office. Another ground rule is that parents should not be allowed to touch you or a teacher in any way. If either of these situations occur, steer the angry parent out of the main office so that the disturbance is not as visible. If these tactics fail to calm the parent or if he or she is on the verge of violence, ask the parent to leave. If that doesn't work, have security escort the parent out. If you don't have security, get help or call the police.

The same holds true for contact over the phone. When a parent starts using abusive language over the phone, simply tell the parent that you will be glad to continue the conversation when they can talk in a reasonable manner. Life is much too short to put up with this sort of nonsense.

The next step in dealing with parents is usually to bring the teacher into the conference. Many school problems involve a student and a particular teacher. Oftentimes the parent has only been told an extremely edited version from the student's perspective of the incident in question. Once the teacher is given the opportunity to relate the full story, the situation can usually be cleared up very quickly.

Remember to always be fair and consistent in all of your dealings with parents. Don't give in to an irate parent, just to get rid of them. Heated encounters with parents will only cause trouble later.

STRATEGY #60

Protect your integrity.

In the school administration field and in life in general, it is sometimes the easiest route to tell people what they want to hear, whether it is the truth or not. Sometimes it is possible, either in your professional or personal life, to get away with telling a falsehood to make yourself look better or to get someone off your back, but lying is never an acceptable practice. Administrators make mistakes and things happen that are often not the principals fault, but a successful principal must admit when something has gone wrong and move on from there. The community will respect a principal who admits when something has gone wrong much more than someone who tries to cover things up. As previously mentioned, school administration is very political and politics are full of examples of officials, such as Bill Clinton and Richard Nixon, who lied, shaded the truth, or tried to cover things up.

Once a school principal gets the reputation of not always telling the truth, every comment and every action will be suspect. If you are always truthful and treat people fairly and consistently, people will always have respect for you, and having the respect of the community is a large part of being a successful principal. People will not always agree with what you say or do, but they will respect what you do.

Also, there is more to protecting your integrity than just always telling the truth. If you say that you are going to do something, make sure that you do what you say. As principal, one of the best things people can say about you is that you are a person of your word.

STRATEGY #61

Develop a thick skin.

Being a school principal is similar in some ways to being a politician, a football coach, or a religious leader in that people in the community love to talk about and criticize the performance of people in these positions. Principals need to realize that fact up front and be prepared to deal with the criticism, be confident in their actions, and not worry about people making derogatory remarks.

Much of what has been discussed in this manuscript is in reference to shaping the public's perceptions of the principal's performance, as this perception is crucial to a school's success. However, principals cannot satisfy all of the people all of the time, and there will be times when principals have to make hard, unpopular decisions. Making the hard decisions is what we get paid for. If you do your job right, you will, by necessity, make some people angry with you. For example, parents very seldom brag about the principal's job performance after their child is suspended from school—the parents of problem children will be the ones who criticize you the most in the community. Teachers sometimes have unreal expectations of principals also and at times want to dictate how a problem should be handled or demand a certain punishment. That sort of thing is not their responsibility, and when they don't get their way it can lead them to criticize the administration. As principal, don't worry about "sour grapes." The challenge is to make sure that you are doing your job to the best of your ability. Always listen to any criticism that you are aware of because someone might have a valid point for you to address. But don't lose any sleep over people talking behind your back. It comes with the territory.

STRATEGY #62

Don't be afraid to move.

Even if a principal follows every recommendation in this book, there will come a time in the career of most principals that it will be time to move on, either to change districts or change jobs. Even though a principal carries out all the duties of the position in a competent, professional manner, problems can still occur. School boards and superintendents can sometimes have different agendas that have nothing to do with how well a person does the job. When you are dealing with elected superintendents and school boards, politics definitely plays a huge role in selecting and retaining school administrators. Even with appointed school superintendents and school boards, politics can still be a problem. Who selects these positions when they are appointed? Other elected officials such as the local board of aldermen, the town council, or the county board of supervisors. As long as that is the case, politics will always be a problem in the schools. Elected officials often have personal or political agendas that affect schools and their personnel but are not based on what is best for the school or its students.

What does this mean for the school principal? This is the environment that principals have to work in, which means they should always be aware of the big picture. How well principals survive the political part of the job will determine how long they stay in a particular position. Am I telling principals to cater to certain groups? No, I am not. However, I am saying not to be stupid and bury your head in the sand. Always be aware of the political ramifications of your actions. Accommodate people when you can. If you ignore the political side, you can get blindsided some-times. Be smarter than that, and try to accommodate and compromise as often as possible so that everyone is happy.

STRATEGY #63

Keep current with technological and administrative innovations.

In the 1990s there were several major changes in education in the United States. One was the change from the traditional six- or seven-period school day to some form of the block schedule at many high schools and middle schools across the country. Another major change was the advent of new technology in education. In our schools today, computers and other forms of technology like graphing calculators that were unheard of twenty years ago are used on a daily basis. Tech-nology is used by teachers to enhance instruction in the classroom, by students to do research and help work math problems, and by admin-istrators to do all the administrative tasks, like attendance, that we used to do with paper and pencil. The Internet alone has radically changed education. Teachers can pull up lesson plans for their course in a mat-ter of minutes. Students can go online and research any area or seek help with any subject. Most schools have Internet access, and many schools have the Internet available in every classroom.

It is the school's responsibility not only to provide these new tech-nologies, but also to provide classes for students to make sure they are all computer literate and to provide some technical training for those students wanting to pursue careers in the technology field.

In order to manage a school with all of this new technological re-sponsibility, the principal must stay current with educational advances in technology. My first experience with a computer came my first day on the job as an assistant principal. I walked into my new office and found a computer on my desk, which I was to use to keep track of my discipline reports. I literally did not know how to turn it on. A lot of administrators and teachers probably had similar experiences over the last decade. Now, there are many steps a principal can follow to stay technologically current:

1. Use the technology yourself. E-mail your faculty. Do PowerPoint presentations for your staff.

2. Work closely with you district's technology staff.

3. Attend technology training for principals.

4. Provide quality training for your staff.

5. Make it a point to visit other schools and school districts to observe what they are doing with technology and borrow good ideas.

6. Evaluate your staff on their use of technology.

Remember technology is very expensive and decisions concerning it's use need to be planned with a good deal of thought and care.

STRATEGY #64

Learn to delegate.

Many principals have aggressive take-charge personalities, which is often why they became principals in the first place. However, with hundreds or even thousands of students and large numbers of teachers to supervise, it is almost impossible to survive without budgeting your time and delegating some of the numerous responsibilities that go along with the job.

How administrative duties are divided is often left up to the individual schools and principals. Some states mandate a certain number of administrators for a specific number of students. For example, a school with 600 or more students might be required to have a principal and one assistant principal. I was personally involved with a school of 1,100 students that only had a principal and assistant principal. Having that small a number of administrators saves the school district money for salaries and looks good politically, but it stretches the administration way too thin. How is having a small number of principals good for political purposes? Some school superintendents try to impress the voters and community with how little of the total school budget is spent on the administration. But, at the same time, you do want to have enough administrators to get the job done well. Piling too much work on too few administrators is one of the reasons it is hard to keep good principals from retiring early when they are at the peak of their abilities. One administrator for every 250 students is a very workable number.

Regardless of the number of administrators at a school, the administrative duties need to be formally divided. This is the principal's responsibility most of the time and should be divided fairly and logically. The following is a sample responsibility chart for a grades seven to twelve high school with 1,500 students and four principals.

Administrative Duties

1. *Principal*—Overall responsibility for the whole school, supervision of assistant principals and teachers, overall responsibility for discipline, instructional leader, curriculum coordinator, shared extracurricular duties.

2. *Assistant Principal 1*—Responsible for discipline of grades 7 and 8, staff development, shared extracurricular duties.

3. *Assistant Principal 2*—Responsible for discipline of grades 9 and 10, textbooks, shared extracurricular duties.

4. *Assistant Principal 3*—Responsible for discipline of grades 11 and 12, substitute teachers, shared extracurricular duties.

For a school of 1,500 students, four is probably the minimum number of administrators required to keep the school running properly. Depending on funding availability, a curriculum specialist and an additional assistant principal would be of immense help.

One last piece of advice for principals is to hire quality assistant principals, give them specific responsibilities, and expect outstanding performance. But always remember, assistant principals and teachers need to know that their principal works as hard or harder than they do.

SUGGESTED ACTIVITIES FOR CHAPTER 6

1. During a regular school day, take a notebook with you during a walk around campus and write down the names of all of the students you encounter who you already know by name. Bring the number of students that you knew plus the total enrollment of your school to the next class meeting. The list can be the basis for a discussion about how well administrators know their students.

2. Briefly describe how faculty meetings are conducted at your school.

3. Bring a copy of your school's student handbook to the next class meeting. Swap handbooks and find a policy in the new handbook you don't agree with or you think could be a potential problem.

4. Research two recent court cases involving education. Write a one-page summary of each, and be prepared to discuss both cases with the class.

5. Make a list of strategies used to deal with irate parents.

APPENDIX

Finding a program to help improve academic performance in our classrooms is something that all principals will be looking at in the near future. Educators will not be able to just keep doing the same old thing. Part of this is due to all of the emphasis, right or wrong, on testing. Some of the change will be driven by our changing society. The following is a list of some of the programs, and their web addresses, that can be used for academic improvement. A complete list with addresses and phone numbers can be found in *Selecting School Reform Models: A Reference Guide for States*, published by

> The Education Commission of the States
> 701 17th Street, Suite 2700
> Denver, CO
> 303-299-3600
> Fax # 303-296-8332
> E-mail ecs@ecs.org
> www.ecs.org

1. Accelerated Schools Project—www-leland.stanford.edu/ group/ASP

2. America's Choice School Design—http://www.ncee.org

3. Atlas Communities—www.edc.org/FSC/ATLAS

4. Coalition of Essential Schools—www.essentialschools.org

5. Community for Learning—http://www.temple.edu/LSS

6. Co-nect Schools—http://co-nect.com

7. Core Knowledge—www.coreknowledge.org

8. Different Ways of Knowing—www.dwoknet.galef.org

9. Direct Instruction—http://www.jponline.com

10. EdisonProject—http://www.edisonproject.com

11. Expeditionary Learning Outward Bound—http://hugs1. harvard.edu

12. Foxfire—www.foxfire.org

13. High Schools That Work—http://www.sreb.org

14. High/Scope Educational Research Foundation—www. highscope.org

15. League of Professional Schools—www.coe.uga.edu/lps/

16. Modern Red Schoolhouse Institute—http://www.mrsh.org

17. Montessori—www.ami.edu

18. Onward to Excellence—http://www.nwrel.org/scpd/ote

19. School Development Program—http://info.med.yale.edu/comer

20. Success for All/Roots & Wings—http://successforall.com

21. Talent Development High School with Career Academies— www.csos.jhu.edu

22. Urban Learning Centers—http://www.lalc.K12.ca.us

REFERENCES

Atcheson, K. A., & Gall, M. D. (1997). *Techniques in the clinical supervision of teachers: Preservice and inservice applications* (4th ed.). White Plains, NY: Longman.

Bassinger, J. (2000). Colleges widen alternate routes to teacher certification. *Chronicle of Higher Education* 46 (19): 18–20.

Bear, G. G. (1998). School discipline in the United States. *School Psychology Review* 27: 14–23.

Buckman, D. C., King, B. B., & Ryan, S. (1995). Block scheduling: A means to improve school climate. *NASSP Bulletin* 79 (571): 9–19.

Canady, R. L., & Rettig, M. D. (1992). Restructuring middle level schools to promote equal access. *Schools in the Middle* 1: 20–26.

Canter, L., & Canter, M. (2001). *Assertive discipline: positive behavior management for today's classroom.* Los Angeles, Calif.: Canter and Associates.

Carroll, J. M. (1987). The Copernican Plan: The evolution of a revolution. *Phi Delta Kappan* 76: 104–113.

Clement, M. C. (1995). If you really want to help the new teacher next door. *Clearing House* 69 (1): 40–41.

Clement, M. C. (2000). Just how do you teach someone to be a teacher. *Phi Delta Kappan* 82 (4): 308–309.

Daves, D. P. (1998). The differences in standardized test scores in varied school period configurations (doctoral dissertation, The University of Southern Mississippi, 1998). *Dissertation Abstracts International* 58 (08): 2720.

Dufour, R. P. (1991). *The principal as staff developer*. Bloomington, IN: National Educational Service.

Education Commission of the States (1999). *Selecting school reform models*. Denver, CO: Education Commission of the States.

Elam, S. M., Rose, L. C., & Gallup, A. M. (1996). 28th Phi Delta Kappan Gallup poll of public attitudes toward the public schools. *Phi Delta Kappan* 78: 41–59.

Epstein, J. (1995). Perspectives and previews on research and policy for school, family, and community partnerships. In Booth and Dunn (eds.), *Family-school links: How do they affect educational outcomes?* Hillsdale, NJ: Lawrence Erlbaum Associates.

Fisher, C. W., & Berliner, D. C. (1985). *Perspectives on instructional time*. White Plains, NY: Longman.

Fitzpatrick, J. E., & Moyers, M. (1997). Success and the four block schedule. *NASSP Bulletin* 81: 51–56.

Flaxman, E., & Inger, M. (1992). Parents and schooling in the 1990's. *Principal* 72 (2): 16–18.

Funtwengler, W. J., & Konnert, W. (1982). *Improving school discipline: An administrator's guide*. Boston: Allyn & Bacon.

Glasser, W. (1969). *Schools without feelings*. New York: Harper and Row.

Goldhammer, R., Anderson, R. H., & Krajewski, R. J. (1993). *Clinical supervision: Special methods for the supervision of teachers* (3rd ed.). Fort Worth, TX: Harcourt Brace Jovanovich.

Hackman, D. G. (1995). Improving school climate: Alternate-day block schedule. *Schools in the Middle* 5: 28–33.

Hickman, C. W., Greenwood, G., & Miller, M. D. (1995). High school parent involvement: Relationships with achievement, grade level, sex, and gender. *Journal of Research and Development in Education* 28 (3): 125–34.

Hope, W. C. (1999). Principals' orientation and induction activities as factors in teacher retention. *Clearing House* 73 (1): 54–56.

Increase security and encourage students to use lunch subsidies. (1992). *Curriculum Review* 32 (4): 19.

Kennedy, M. (2001). Discouraging restroom vandalism. *American School & University* 73 (11): 32.

Kerrins, J. A. (2001). Take this job and fill it. *Leadership* 30 (5): 20–23.

Khazzaka, J. (1997). Comparing the merits of a seven period day to those of a four period day. *High School Journal* 81 (2): 87-98

Kohlberg, L. (1970). *Education for justice in moral education.* Cambridge, MA: Harvard University Press.

Klecker, B. M., Austin, J. L, & Burns, L.T. (2000). An in-depth analysis of decisions made by Kentucky's school based decision making councils. *Education* 120 (4): 655-668.

Lee, S. (1994). Family-school connections and student's education: Continuity and change of family involvement for the middle grades to high school. Unpublished dissertation. The Johns Hopkins University.

Lybbert, B. (1998). *Transforming learning with block scheduling: A guide for principals.* Thousand Oaks, CA: Corwin.

Marks, H. M., & Lewis, K. S. (1999). Teacher empowerment and the capacity for organizational learning. *Education Administration Quarterly* 35: 707-48.

Mississippi Department of Education (2001). *Fast Facts: A guide to federal and state programs hused in the office of innovative support.* Jackson, MS: Author.

Morgan, N., & Sprague, C. (2000). Teacher resources. *Teacher Librarian* 28 (1).

O'Neil, J. (1995). Finding time to learn. *Educational Leadership* 53: 11-15.

Partington, G. (1999). Suburban Kansas City schools use ID badges. *American School & University* 71 (11): 14.

Piaget, J. (1932). *The moral judgement of the child.* Glencoe, IL: Free Press.

Popham, W. J. (2001). *The Truth about testing.* Alexandria, VA: Association for Supervision and Curriculum Development.

Potter, L. (1997). Tips for principals. *Education Digest* 63 (1): 58-59.

Queen, J. A., & Gaskey, K. A. (1997). Steps for improving school climate in block scheduling. *Phi Delta Kappan,* 79 (2): 158-162.

Ramirez, A. Y. (2001). Parent involvement is like apple pie: A look at parental involvement in two states. *High School Journal* 85 (1): 1.

Reed, R. J. (1983). Administrators advice: Cause and remedies of school conflict and violence. *NASSP Bulletin* 67: 75-79.

Reutter, E. E. (1994). *The law of public education.* (4th ed.). Westbury, NY: Foundation Press.

Should new teachers get the toughest assignments? (2000). *NEA Today* 18: 11.

Simpson, M. D. (2001). Dress codes are back in style. *NEA Today*, 19 (7): 18.

Snyder, D. (1997). *4 block scheduling: A case study of data analysis of one high school after two years*. Washington, DC: U.S. Department of Education.

Snow, A. L. (2001). Teacher, administrator, and student perception of the impact of block scheduling on high school discipline. Doctoral dissertation, University of Southern Mississippi.

Stanley, S. (1996). School uniforms and safety. *Education & Urban Society*, 28 (4): 424–436.

Ubben, G. C., Hughes, L. W., & Norris, C. J. (2001). *The principal: Creative leadership for effective schools*. Boston: Allyn & Bacon.

U.S. Department of Education. (1996). *The pocket condition of education*. Washington, DC: U.S. Government Printing Office.

U.S. Department of Education. (1998). *Annual report on school safety*. Washington, DC: U.S. Government Printing Office.

Weis, C. (2000). Measuring up: The API as a planning tool. *Thrust for educational leadership* 29 (4): 5.

What the numbers say. (1999). *Curriculum Review* 39 (2): 2.

Wickham, D. (2001). Rethink school zero-tolerance laws. *The Clarion–Ledger*, December 4, 2001, p. 7A.

Wingert, P. (1999). Uniforms rule. *Newsweek* 134 (14): 72–73.

Wood, C. L., Nicholson, E. W., and Findley, D. G. (1985). *The secondary school principal: Manager and supervisor*. Boston: Allyn & Bacon.

Wong, H. K., & Wong, R. T. (1998). *The first days of school*. Mountain View, CA: Harry K. Wong Publications.

ABOUT THE AUTHOR

Albert Lee Snow has been employed in the public and private schools in Mississippi for the past twenty-four years. During that time he has taught on all levels from junior high to college. As an administrator, he has served as a high school assistant principal, an elementary school principal, principal of two different public high schools, and headmaster of a K-12 private school. Dr. Snow received his Doctorate in Education from the University of Southern Mississippi.